I WILL NEVER 'FUR-GET' YOU

SNEHA CHAUDHARY

Copyright © Sneha Chaudhary
All Rights Reserved.

This book has been published with all efforts taken to make the material error-free after the consent of the author. However, the author and the publisher do not assume and hereby disclaim any liability to any party for any loss, damage, or disruption caused by errors or omissions, whether such errors or omissions result from negligence, accident, or any other cause.

While every effort has been made to avoid any mistake or omission, this publication is being sold on the condition and understanding that neither the author nor the publishers or printers would be liable in any manner to any person by reason of any mistake or omission in this publication or for any action taken or omitted to be taken or advice rendered or accepted on the basis of this work. For any defect in printing or binding the publishers will be liable only to replace the defective copy by another copy of this work then available.

In Loving Memory Of Ronnie...

Contents

" Dogs have a way of finding people who need them, and filling emptiness we never thought we had before. "

"No one truly understands the meaning of love unless he has owned a dog. "

" Pets come into our lives to teach us about love, and they depart to teach us about loss. Getting a new pet never replaces the old one, it just expands the heart. "

" When an eighty - five pound mammal licks your tears away and tries to sit on your lap, it's hard to feel sad. "

" Stop telling me that he's just a dog. My dog has more character, loyalty and honesty than most people I know. "

" A Dog is the only thing on Earth that loves you more that he loves himself "

Foreword

Have you ever felt like your whole life was a lie? Like everything you ever believed in, everything you hoped for didn't matter because it was never going to happen?

This story is about a girl named Kacy Snow, a little girl who had always wanted a pet dog but was never able to convince her parents to get one. After a lot of convincing and making a lot of promises, her parents finally agreed on bringing a sweet innocent little puppy home. His name was Ronnie. It was the sweetest and the most surreal thing that happened to her. Every single moment with him somehow made all of her worries disappear. She loved him more than anything she had ever loved. Why wouldn't she? After all he was family...

After Ronnie came in Kacy's life, everything was perfect. It was going pretty well until everything took a really unexpected turn. Will Kacy figure out what actually happened that day or will she just live behind a lie her whole life? Join Kacy Snow in her mysterious yet emotional journey...

This is a non-fintional novel based on the author's real life. It revolves around the idea of what most pet owners go through...

CHAPTER ONE

KACY SNOW

"Okay... don't be mad... but can we please get a puppy? It would be so amazing. We would take him on walks and play fetch. Let's not be the family who has never owned a pet... " said little Kacy Snow while she was watching her favourite cartoon on TV. Not that she hadn't asked the same thing maybe like a million times before. But Mr. and Mrs. Snow never said yes. Instead they said, "We'll get you one when you're grown up and have learned to take care of yourself." Kacy didn't know when that was going to happen. "Grow up? But I am grown up, I'm 6 and in 5 months I'll be 7... please, I promise I'll take care of it with all my love." she said. Her little brother Peter, who was 3 and in nursery, accompanied his sister in requesting their parents. He said in his cute little voice, "Puppie are so cute...we promise we'll take care of it." Still the answer didn't change.

Kacy studies in the first grade. She has always had a great love for dogs. She loves giving biscuits to stray dogs in her neighbourhood. She has always wanted a pet dog but was always denied by her parents to get one. Her mom, Penny Snow and dad, Stephen Snow love her more than anything. Her brother Peter is in kindergarten. And her Grandma is a nurse who works in the hospital im front of their house. The Snows live in the staff quarters of the hospital.

"Grandma, can you please tell mom and dad?" Kacy said thinking grandma will say yes. Because she never denies what Kacy says. But instead she said, "Dear, dogs create a mess in the house and your brother is really young, what if he gets sick because of it? You wouldn't want that. Would you?" Kacy didn't know how to answer that so she just continued watching TV.

She has always wanted a dog. Seeing other people with their pets on TV and outside in parks and streets, made her feel like there was something missing in her life. She used to tell her parents that she won't ask for anything again if they let her have a pet dog. Many kids of her age feel the same. When she was young, well younger than now, she used to draw stuff on a wall. It was really kind of her parents to let her do that. And the drawing she loved the most was the one in which she made a little girl with her dog. Under which she wrote 'I love my pet'. Even though she didn't have one that time. And whenever she saw it, she wished that one day that girl would be her. She wished for it more than anything. It was a dream she thought would never come true. Because her parents never said yes. They always used to say that once she grew up, they wouldn't hesitate into letting her have a dog. No matter how much she requested, nothing seemed to work. It was not that her parents hated animals, they loved them just as much as she did. In fact, before she was born, they had a pet dog named 'Silky' who was a little white pomeranian given to them by one of their neighbours.

Well, the family did bring animals to their house sometimes. The ones they used to rescue or save. But eventually, those animals ended up in a rescue organization. No, rescuing animals wasn't their job or something. But they just did it because of, as mentioned before, their love for animals.

There was this one time when they went to have dinner at a relatives' house. It was raining a lot that night. When they came back home, they saw there was a little kitten shivering on the corner street near their block. It must have probably gotten separated from its parents. Mr. Snow loved animals just as Kacy did. It was just because of Penny, that he said no. Because she already did a lot around the house and he didn't want to give her more stress. Plus, they had a busy schedule.

The kitten was making noises because it felt cold and the rain wasn't stopping. So they decided to take the kitten inside their house. They dried it off with a towel. And then fed it and gave it warm milk to drink. Both the children loved playing with it as it was so cute and little. They even made a little bed for the kitty in a cardboard box where it slept for the night..

The next day they woke up to check up on the kitty. The living room was a whole mess. The curtains were torn, grandma's favourite vase was broken and the frames had scratches on it. No wonder it was done by the little innocent looking kitty. When they looked inside the box, the kitten wasn't there. So they started looking around. The little kitten was sleeping under the couch. It would obviously be impossible to keep that kitten inside the house. So they decided to send the kitty to a rescue organization.

The family used to live in staff quarters of the hospital where grandma worked. There was a temple called 'Kirti Mandir' beside the quarters. There were some people there who used to take care of the rescued cats and dogs. So they sent the cat there.

Anyways, at least Kacy got to experience what it's like to have a pet even if it wasn't a dog. Not that she didn't like cats, but Kacy had a different love for dogs. Well, it was always a no from mom and dad so...

The next month, Mr. Snow along with Kacy's cousin brother, Matt, who was 14, brought a stray puppy home. He lived in the quarters of the same hospital beside Kacy's house because his mom, Kacy's aunt also worked in the same hospital. He was, just like Kacy, obsessed with dogs. But his mom, Beth, was terrified of dogs. So, Matt directly brought the dog to Mr. Snow. The puppy was hurt and was making little noises which dogs usually make when they're crying, when Matt found it while playing with his friends in the neighbourhood. Matt saw a collar on its neck. "Romeo!" he said, showing the collar, "this dog's name is Romeo." They decided to bring it home as it was seriously injured.

After they brought it home, they mended its wounds and fed it. It had a really deep cut on it's left back leg. The blood was dried but somehow Mrs. Snow was able to clean it. The puppy was of a combination of brown, white and black colour. And cuteness overload. It seemed like it was trained too as it sat on command and did different tricks too. His fur was filled with dirt. It was a mess, no wonder that it had rolled in a puddle. As it was a rainy day. After all it was a little puppy who obviously wouldn't have known how to live alone. After cleaning it and all, the next question was where to send him because the rescue organization which was in the temple beside had transferred somewhere else.

"So what are we going to do with him now?" asked Mr. Snow.

"Someone must have lost it. And would be looking for it" said Mrs. Snow.

"Yeah, the owners must be worried. I'll send a photo of him to the police station. If the owner comes looking for it, they'll inform us."

"So what are we going to do till we find the owner?"

"Let's keep him till then. Kids will love spending time with it."

The kids got so excited when they heard this conversation.

They had so much fun with Romeo. They made him play catch with Matt's light green tennis ball. It was such a great day that no one knew how time flew by...

The next day, Kacy went to school. During classes, the only thing that was on her mind the whole time was that she would get to play with Romeo after school ends. When she reached home, she saw that dad and Peter weren't home and Romeo wasn't too.

"Where's Romeo?" she asked mom hesitantly.

"He's with your dad and Peter on the main ground." replied Mrs. Snow.

"Well then, I'm also going with them."

"First change your uniform and then you can go."

Then Kacy went inside and changed her uniform as fast as she could. Then she went to the ground where she saw them. Mr. Snow, Peter and Matt were playing with Romeo.

She joined them. After some time, a call came on dad's phone. After hanging it up, he said, "They have found the owner of Romeo and they'll come to take him in the evening." The kids were really sad on hearing this. They were happy too because Romeo will finally be with his owners. So they played with Romeo as much as they could because there were very few chances that they would get to meet him again.

At 5PM a guy with dark brown curly hair, with a yellow t-shirt, probably 21, came at the front door. Kacy had never seen that guy so she called her parents.

"I'm here for Romeo. I'm his owner." said the boy.

"Yeah my nephew found him on the street the other day and he was hurt so he directly brought him here." said Mr. Snow.

"Thank you so much for taking care of him. I don't know how to tell you how grateful I am. I thought I would never get to see him again." the boy said.

"How did you lose him?"

"We were out for our usual walk. And suddenly a call came from my mom saying that we ran out of milk. So I decided to stop at a grocery shop as we walked past it. It was a little supermarket kind of shop so the bill counter was inside. When I entered the shop, the security told me that the shop had a strict no pets rule. So I tied Romeo's leash outside the shop. But somehow it managed to get loose, and the next thing I know is that I lost him."

"He was even hurt. You should take care of him"

Then dad went inside to get Romeo...

As soon as Romeo saw the boy, it took off from dad's arms in a tremendous leap and sailed into the boy's lap. He gave a startled "Ooh!" And then had to defend himself as Romeo swarmed over him, licking his face and barking. This made Kacy realize that Romeo would be much happier with his owner. Till then she was just picturing the guy as a monster who came to take away Romeo. As much as it hurt, Kacy knew it was for the best. She hugged him while her parents were talking to that owner. And then Romeo and his owner went on their way...

CHAPTER TWO

WELCOME HOME, RONNIE

It was a normal day in the house. Kacy and Peter were playing with mom and dad. And grandma was watching the news on TV. And everything was going perfectly fine. After the news was finished, grandma gave the remote to Mr. Snow. He turned the National Geographic Channel on and guess what... the show in which funny videos of animals are shown, was going on. Mr. and Mrs. Snow saw it coming and there it was. "Aww... these puppies are so... cute, only if we had one, I would know what it's like to have a pet." But this was all normal. They were all used to it.

Suddenly the doorbell rang. Mr.and Mrs. Snow were relieved because they didn't want to hear Kacy go on again about getting a pet.

"Kacy, go and check who's at the door" said Mrs. Snow.

she got up to open the door. It was aunt Beth and Matt!

"Why aren't you guys ready yet?" said Aunt Beth.

"We were supposed to go to the park...don't tell me you forgot. "

"Yeah it completely slipped my mind" said Mr. Snow.

Kacy and Peter got really excited because they hadn't been to the park for months. They both got ready as fast as they could. Then the parents also got ready.

After getting ready, everyone sat in the car and were off to the park. Grandma stayed at home. They walked in the garden for a little while and then all of them went in the toy train which takes a round around the whole park including the zoo too. Even though it's called a toy train, it is made for both kids and adults. Then the kids started playing on the slides and swings, while the elders were talking...

"Stephen, do you happen to know any pet store owners." asked aunt Beth.

"I think I may have some in my contacts, I'll check. Why, what happened?" said Mr. Snow.

"The thing is that recently, Matt has been going on and off about getting a dog. I'm just getting sick of his tantrums." said aunt Beth.

"What kind of dog does he want?"

"Labrador. But the thing is that I'm terrified of dogs and you know that very well."

"Yeah, do you know the real reason why she never used to come to Aunt Bertha's house whenever they invited us to have dinner together?" Stephen asked Penny.

"Because their son had adopted a pomeranian dog and it used to bark a lot when any guests came to the house." he added with a laugh.

" Well then how will you adopt one if you're so scared?" asked Penny.

"Exactly" said Aunt Beth

"How am I supposed to take care of a dog'?" she added.

"Don't worry, you'll get used to it by time." said Stephen.

"Let's hope"

Then it was time to get back home. Matt, Peter and Kacy got off the swings and they were on their way back home.

A few days later, Mr.Snow called Aunt Beth on the phone.

"Hello"

"Hello, hey Stephen, how are ya?"

"I'm good. Listen , I've been searching for some pet stores since last week, and there's this one store called 'Pet Spot'. We can go and see whenever we're free."

"Ok I'll check my schedule and we'll go."

A few days later, on 15th October, they finally decided to go to the shop. Kacy was so excited and because she knew that she would get to play with a puppy everyday as it'll be living in her Aunt's house. So she got ready before everyone.

On the way Kacy said, "Dad if we're going to the pet shop to buy a dog for Matt then can we also get one together?" "No dear, let Matt get his puppy today, and we'll get one later. Till then we'll play with Matt's puppy, okay." replied Mr. Snow.

The final shop everyone decided from which they wanted to get the puppy was called 'Pet Spot'. There were little paws drawn beside the title. While they were entering the shop, a family had just got out with their new puppy. Kacy just couldn't hold her excitement while entering. The same excitement was of Mr. Snow who had decided to take one puppy home as soon as he entered.

The shop had that puppy smell that every dog owner must be very familiar with. Different types of chew toys and dog foods were on the shelves which were on the walls. There were dog collars and leashes on the stands in the inner part of the shop. There were 3 little Labrador Retriever puppies in the middle of the room and a fully grown Rottweiler was sleeping beside the counter. The shopkeeper, Mr. Cooper was a decent kind looking man wearing a cap which had a title of the store. There was one more shelf beside the counter. It had 3 transparent glass boxes on it. Each box had one little hamster inside it. They were really adorable. Mr. Snow and Matt even took one in their hands. It's fur was really soft, it felt like a cottenball in their hands.

When Aunt Beth saw the puppies. She thought to herself, "How am I supposed to take care of the dog and Matt both. I barely get enough time to spend with Matt because of work."

Suddenly she said to Matt, "I'm sorry dear, but we'll not be buying a puppy today. I don't think I'll be able to raise it." Then Mr. Snow asked, "Why not?" Aunt Beth looked at the puppies and said, "Just no, there's no way I'm letting a dog inside my home."

"Okay if you're not buying then we'll get one. Kacy has also been asking for it for a long time." Mr. Snow said, looking at Mrs. Snow. Bringing Kacy up was just an excuse, the real reason was that Mr. Snow just wanted a puppy just as badly as Kacy. "What!" said Mrs. Snow in great astonishment. Mr. Snow said, "Trust me, we'll take care of it with all of our heart." As soon as Kacy heard this, she said, "Yes mom, you won't have to do anything." "Don't you think this is a bit fast to take such a huge decision...Fine, but don't forget your responsibilities." said Mrs. Snow. Her heart was also melted when she saw those puppies. On hearing this Kacy and Peter jumped out of excitement. Matt was also happy, thinking even though he didn't get a puppy of his own, at least he'll get to play with it. This was the best conversation that Kacy had ever had in her while life. It all felt surreal to her. She just couldn't believe that it was actually happening.

The three Labrador puppies were siblings, two brothers and a sister. The sister and one of the brothers were sleeping, while the other one who was quite energetic, was jumping on them and running and just didn't stop. Then it went to the Rottweiler who was sleeping right beside the counter. It looked a bit dangerous. But it didn't affect the puppy at all, instead it just kept on running around it. This made Mr. Snow realize that it's the puppy that they want to adoptener, the most energetic little one . So he told the shopkeeper to keep the papers of adoption ready. Then he told the family that the puppy that they're going to adopt is the one who's jumping and running around the whole place. Everyone was extremely happy.

Kacy just couldn't believe that this was really happening. Two hours ago she was convinced that she's never going to get a pet dog and now everything is upside down. She just knew that this was the best moment of her life.

It was so cute, so little. Just a month old. Just playing and tumbling on the floor. With little golden between the skin colored hair. Just like every other Labrador Retriever. He even had a little red wet nose. It's black-brown paws were really soft. But there was something different about it, Kacy fell in love with it the moment she laid her eyes on it, the moment her life changed. She just knew that it was one of the most important people in her life. The joy that she felt was indescribable. It was like the drawing that she did on that wall was somehow the prediction of the future. She just couldn't stop smiling.

"Good things need patience, they take time to happen. But great things happen at the most unexpected times..."

When Mr. Snow took the puppy in his hands, Kacy went near it and touched it, gliding her hands from its head. It's fur was so soft and smooth. It was so delicate and innocent who didn't even know what was going on . Then Mrs. Snow took it in her hands. It immediately started licking her face. "Looks like it really likes you" said Mr. Snow. Then Matt took him in his hands. Surprisingly, aunt Beth took some courage and touched it. When they told Peter to touch it, he got a little scared but still did so, softly. Kacy wanted to take the puppy in her hands too but she was afraid that it would fall off her hands.

The shopkeeper brought the adoption papers and placed them on the counter. After Mr. Snow filled all the papers. The puppy was finally adopted. Its birth date was 13th September 2013. Which made it exactly a month and two days old.

Before leaving the shop, they also bought a bowl for dog food. It was a metal bowl with black rubber strip around its edge. Then an orange rubber chew toy shaped like a ball. It had little spikes on it. They didn't get a leash for it because the puppy was too small for leashes.

Afterwards, it was finally the time to bring the puppy home. As Mr. Snow was driving, Mrs. Snow had the puppy in her hands. It fell asleep as it was tired because of playing. "Mom? Can I please have him in my lap." asked Kacy. "Sure thing dear" replied Mrs. Snow lifting the puppy up and placing it on Kacy's lap. It woke up for a few seconds but fell asleep again. "Are you happy now? Finally..." asked mom. "More than you can imagine" Kacy said, smiling.

Before reaching home, they stopped at a temple to get a *pooja* done for the newest member of the family. The *pandit* did a small *tilak* on the puppy's forehead with *kumkum*. Then all of them were on their way home.

Everyone forgot to inform grandma, so it was a total surprise for her when they reached home. The puppy was a little scared in the beginning as it was around new people. But in no amount of time, it started playing around. "Dad? What will we call him?" asked Kacy. "What do you want to call him?" asked Mr. Snow. Suddenly Peter replied, "Tommy! We'll call him Tommy." Then Matt said, "Bruno is much better." Everyone started suggesting one by one. "Oscar..., Stan..." and the suggestions continued. Mr. Snow was looking up on the internet for some good names. "How about 'Ronnie'?" He added. And everyone's face was lit up with smiles. "Sounds nice" said Mrs. Snow. It was the first name that everyone agreed on. So there it was.

Little Ronnie seemed to love his new home. He immediately got along with Kacy and Peter. Then he roamed th whole house as if he was checking out his new home. It was so... adorable.

Then Mr. Snow and Matt went to get some dog food for Ronnie. The shop keeper had told them that Ronnie should be fed celerac which is technically baby food. They added a little water to it as followed from the instructions. And then put it in the bowl. Ronnie ate it in no time as he was really hungry. The food was stuck on Ronnie's nose. So Kacy brought a little cloth to clean

it up. Then Ronnie was active again and started playing with Kacy. Mr. and Mrs. Snow felt so happy seeing that smile on her face. They thought that the one thing that was missing in their life was Ronnie. Their family was finally complete.

Then they saw a little water on the floor. "It's not water, I guess it was done by the puppy". Kacy immediately went inside, brought the mop and started mopping. Because she wanted to show her parents how responsible she was.

Then Aunt Beth and Matt left. Peter was small so he felt a little bit scared of Ronnie. He used to run away from him while Ronnie ran behind him. Then Ronnie felt tired again. They put a small mattress on the floor so that he won't catch a cold. But instead, Ronnie just kept on climbing out of it because the floor felt much better as it was cool.

In the evening, everyone was tired, so they were laying down on the bed. Ronnie was sleepy too. So he went close to Mrs. Snow and slept in her arms. So that he would feel safe. It was really adorable.

At night, grandma slept in her room as usual. While the other 4 usually sleep on a double bed together. The question now was 'Where will Ronnie sleep?' So. They made a little bed for him in a box and placed it on the bed with them. And he slept safe and sound in it.

This day was a highlight in Kacy's life. She just couldn't be happier. It was a highlight for the whole family. Their life was filled with happiness. The happiness that came in the most unexpected way...

CHAPTER THREE

LITTLE MOMENTS

Kacy was so pumped up, no matter how tired she was she just couldn't fall asleep. Every now and then she got up and took a look at Ronnie. She slid her little hands on his head which woke him up a bit but Kacy just couldn't help it. Eventually, she finally fell asleep as it had been a very long day.

The next morning, Ronnie was the first to wake up. His delicate little bark woke everyone up extcept Kacy. Then Mrs. Snow went to the kitchen and gave Ronnie his food. Turned out her guessing was correct, Ronnie was barking because he was hungry. Then after some time Kacy woke up. When she saw Ronnie eating, her face lit up with a smile. She had completely forgotten that she had finally got a pet dog. It felt unbelievable.

Luckily, it was a non instructional day at school, so Kacy was at home. But Peter had to go. So Mr. Snow went to drop him. Then Penny took some photos of Kacy with Ronnie. Which turned our really cute.

Grandma was making tea in the kitchen. Ronnie could smell it right from the living room so he ran directly to where the smell was coming from. Grandma didn't know that he had come. He suddenly started licking grandma's feet. Grandma wasn't used to Ronnie. After all, it had only been a day. Suddenly she shouted and Ronnie got scared and took a few steps back. Penny and Kacy just couldn't stop laughing. "Grandma, it was just Ronnie, there's no reason to be scared." Grandma was a bit scared of the puppy at first. She used to climb up on the bed whenever Ronnie was in the room. But eventually she also got attached to him. She wasn't scared anymore.

After dropping Peter off at school, Mr. Snow came back home. The doorbell rang and Ronnie went running to the door. Then Kacy went to open it. It was dad. As soon as he entered, Ronnie started juming with joy. He went behind him wherever he went. So finally, Mr. Snow took Ronnie in his hands. It started licking his face as if it was meeting him after days. It was so little that it fit right between Mr. Snow's hands. Then they decided to make him play with the rubber spike ball which they had bought from the pet shop the other day. Ronnie loved it. For a little puppy, with little legs and paws, he was really fast. He got so excited that he just didn't stop running behind the ball. Those were some really fun minutes of entertainment for the family. Ronnie just couldn't get enough of that ball. Him tumbling and getting up again made it even more adorable to watch.

After Peter came home it was time to finally time to make him overcome his fear from Ronnie. So after he went and changed his uniform. Kacy picked Ronnie up and placed it on Peter's lap. Ronnie was a little tired so luckily he didn't start moving fast. Or else Peter would've gotten scared. But Ronnie repeatedly got off of Peter's lap because he wanted to sleep. So he finally fell asleep on the floor. That time Peter finally touched Ronnie. As it would not move much. Mrs. Snow immediately clicked a photo as it was the first time Peter got along with Ronnie.

In the afternoon while the whole family was having rest in the other room, Kacy decided to spend some time with Ronnie. Because he was all awake as he had just woken up. Kacy made him run behind her. And stopped sometimes when she wanted to pet him. Then she went to get her stuffed ball. Well, it was a ball but made in a way how stuffed toys are made. It had different colours on it. So Kacy thought that Ronnie would like it. And he seemed to have quite an interest in it. Because he just didn't stop. The main task that he wanted to complete was to get the ball in his mouth. But it was too big for him. So he went wherever the ball rolled. Kacy had so much fun watching Ronnie play. It was a bit difficult at first but then finally, Ronnie was able to hold the ball with his mouth. Well he was just able to hold the cloth with his teeth but it seemed like a victory to Ronnie. So as soon as the task was complete, he started moving his head from left to right and then right to left simultaneously holding the ball. His excitement was indescribable. The next second Kacy realised that the ball was stuck in his teeth. So she immediately held him in her hands and no matter how difficult it was, she managed to hold him still and get the ball out of his teeth. Then eventually he got tired. So Kacy went to her room and brought a pillow for her and laid down right beside Ronnie. It was such a precious moment. It was the golden hour of the day so the golden sunlight was falling right on her and Ronnie through the window. Half n' hour later, Kacy woke up when Ronnie started licking her face. And it was definitely the best way she had ever woken up.

"Kacy! Your friends are here." said grandma opening the door of the balcony. Kacy's friends were shouting and calling her to play. She and her friends used to play together every evening. And never skipped a day. It was like a regular routine which never went out of order. Except for you know, whenever they were out. Kacy used to finish her homework directly after coming from school just so that her mom would let her go play with her friends in the evening. But this time when grandma told her that her friends were calling her, she didn't want to go to play for the first time. Just so she could play with Ronnie. Her parents and grandma were so surprised.

"Grandma, please tell them that I won't go to play today..." Kacy said to grandma. "But why dear?" asked grandma. She was quite surprised because Kacy never refused to go to play with her friends. "I want to spend time with Ronnie today." Kacy replied. Before grandma reached the balcony to tell Kacy's friends, a thought struck her and she immediately ran to the balcony to tell her friends about Ronnie. All of them were so excited to play with him. Then they went inside the house. Ronnie was a bit scared at first, because he had never been with so many people at once. So it took some time for him to get along with the other kids. All of Kacy's friends were so happy to play with Ronnie. Little Ronnie also seemed to love the company of new kids. Millie, who was Kacy's best friend in the group, was really excited because now they had finally got a new character in the game they have been playing for years. It was more like a role play game which they made by themselves.

A little while later after Kacy's friends had left, her Aunt Rose along with Kacy's cousins Molly and Kevin came. Who also live in the same society as theirs. Aunt Rose is a nurse in the neurological ward. Molly is 13 and Kevin is 8. Kevin was exactly 2 years older than Kacy. They share their birthday on November 1st. Where one was born in 2006 and the other was born in 2004. They had come to play with the newest member of the family. After playing with

Ronnie, Molly and Kevin went to play video games with Peter. They were teaching him a new game on the computer they have been playing for weeks.

That time Mr. Snow was talking to aunt Rose in the living room. Mr. Snow and Kacy were sitting on the bed and Aunt Rose was sitting on a chair beside it. While on the bed, Kacy had Ronnie on her lap. She had held him so that he would run away. On one end, the adults were talking and on the other, Kacy was playing with Ronnie. Somehow Ronnie managed to get off of Kacy's hands and suddenly started running. Before Kacy could even realize what had happened, Ronnie ran to the end of the bed and fell between a small space between the bed and the coffee table. The exact time when Kacy heard Ronnie whine, it felt like somebody stabbed her heart with a knife. When they heard a thud of Ronnie falling, everyone turned around and Mr. Snow got up immediately to pick up Ronnie. Kacy was so worried. She had never been this worried in her whole life. Of course nothing seemed to happen to Ronnie because he had started playing again. But Kacy was in a whole different state of mind. She just couldn't help but blame herself for what happened. Her parents told her that there's no need to worry but that didn't change anything. Because Kacy knew if she hadn't let Ronnie get loose, he wouldn't have gotten hurt. Then she decided to play with Ronnie on the floor. So that he doesn't get hurt again. Poor Kacy just couldn't stop thinking about what happened. She thought that it was just the second day with Ronnie and he already got hurt because of her.

The next day, Mrs. Snow woke Kacy up at 6 AM. Because Kacy had to go to school. Kacy sat with Ronnie for a little while, and then got up to get ready. It was just a matter of time when Kacy's Rickshaw uncle who usually takes Kacy to school started shouting her name from the outside. Kacy wasn't the only one coming in the rickshaw. Some of her schoolmates who lived in the same area also came in the same rickshaw. Kacy couldn't wait to tell her friends at school about Ronnie.

After school, when they came home. Kacy's school friends from the rickshaw came inside her house to play with Ronnie. All the kids had so much fun.

Spending time with Ronnie had become Kacy's favorite part of the day. It is the reason she looked forward to come home from school everyday. Good thing is that it didn't affect her studies even a little bit. Because her parents told her that if her grades get lower because of Ronnie then they'll send him back to the shop. Of course they weren't going to do it. It was just to keep Kacy grounded.

Dog's grow way faster than human beings. That's why Ronnie was getting bigger day by day. Slowly 2 weeks went by. He slowly started to become too big for the box he used to sleep in every night. One day when everyone was left to wake up, Ronnie got out of the box and started to lick Mr. Snow's feet. Which of course woke him up. The very day, him and Mrs. Snow went to the pet store to get a proper bed for Ronnie to sleep in. They brought a big blue rectangular basket like bed. It was thrice the size of Ronnie. He loved it.

Ronnie also had a chair of his own. It was a caramel brown plastic chair. He loved sitting on it and scratching its plastic arms. He used to bite the chair and scratch his nails on it. They had not bought the chair specifically for Ronnie, but he seemed to love spending time on it. So it was officially his. One day, while they were having breakfast in the bedroom, suddenly a sound of Ronnie whining came from the living room. So they immediately ran towards the living room to see what had happened. Ronnie was sitting on his chair and his tail was somehow under one of the chair's leg. Mr. Snow immediately got Ronnie out of the chair. No one knew how Ronnie had goten himself into such a surprising position. Poor baby.

One day when Mrs. Snow was making Peter do his homework, Kacy was doing her homework too. Mr. Snow wasn't at home, grandma had gone to meet one of the relatives and Ronnie was sleeping in the very same room. Everyone was busy with something when suddenly Mrs. Snow realized that Ronnie wasn't there. "Kacy, go and check where Ronnie is." she said. "He was just here. I'll go check." When Kacy went inside, Ronnie was by the bathroom. Kacy immediately took Ronnie up and brought him back to the living room. "He was by the bathroom." she said. "Don't let him go back there, or else he'll get sick." said Mrs. Snow.

From that day, they used to put Ronnie's bed to block the area with his crate-bed from where he would be able to go to different places like the bathroom. After Mr. Snow came home, they decided to make Ronnie wear one of Peter's T-shirts. It was a red, blue and white striped t-shirt. It took some effort to make Ronnie wear it. But it was all worth it.it was the cutest thing ever... Well he was having a little difficulty in walking at first because of it. But then he got used to it. He looked so adorable in that little t-shirt. It was the best.

The next day, in the evening, the children were playing with Ronnie in the bedroom while Mrs. Snow had kept Ronnie's dog food in warmed water as it was instructed for the puppies. Then Ronnie fell asleep, so both the children started playing video games on the computer. Then Ronnie suddenly woke up with that smell of his food. The smell was coming right from the kitchen. So he went directly there. And searched for it for a while. Because the bowl was closed with a plate. When he finally figured out where it was, he slowy slid the plate aside and started eating his food. Yes, Ronnie was also getting naughtier and naughtier day by day. When Mrs. Snow saw that, she felt surprised too. Anyways it was the time to feed him so she didn't say anything. This same situation happened several times with cured too. Well she did show it to the kids. They were surprised by Ronnie's keen ability to smell and find stuff. Ronnie also loved eating curd. It was kinda his favorite thing to eat. He loved it even more than his own food. So every time they brought curd home. They brought a little extra specially for Ronnie.

It had been 3 weeks with Ronnie, so they finally decided to buy a leaash for him. It was a brown color belt which they bought. Everyone was making some really sweet memories with Ronnie. They used to go to Aunt Beth's every week. Take Ronnie for a walk. And have so much fun with him. All of Kacy's neighborhood friends also loved to play with Ronnie. It was so perfect.

One normal evening, the family was playing with Ronnie in the bedroom. He was tied to his leash. It was a bit late, so they decided to have dinner. They left Ronnie tied to his leash in the bedroom while they were having dinner in the dining room. Suddenly, Ronnie came running from the bedroom to the dining room. It made everyone wonder how he managed to get off his leash. So they immediately went inside the room and what they saw was pretty unbelievable. Ronnie had broken the belt just by biting it every now and then. It is the reason why he was able to get off his leash. Everyone started laughing the second they realized that. "I guess we're going to have to buy a strongerleash for Ronnie." said Mr. Snow.

When Ronnie became 8 weeks old, it was time to start it's vaccination. When the doctor came, he made them fill some forms. Then it was time for the vaccine. At first Kacy thought that it was no big deal but when the doctor pricked Ronnie, he whined. It was hurting Ronnie but it was hurting Kacy more seeing him cry that way. But there was nothing she could do because vaccines are a must. However, it was a huge relief after the doctor finally left.

Peter had a stuffed pug. So a couple days ago they had given it to Ronnie to play. However, Peter was bored with it so he didn't mind. Then Ronnie had started ripping it off. You know with puppies, whenever they find a new thing, it first goes in their mouth. And it only took one week for Ronnie to completely rip it off until all the stuffing got out. It did create a lot of mess. But the one thing that affected Peter more than the mess was the fact that his stuffed toy was gone forever. He cried a lot even though he said that it was okay to give it to Ronnie. He also got angry but eventually got over it. After all, there was nothing he could've done.

One beautiful Sunday morning. The sun was shining brightly and everything was going on as usual. Kacy and Peter were still sleeping, Mom and dad were having their morning tea. And grandma was heading to the balcony to get the newspaper. The man who delivers the newspaper usually drops it in their balcony. He had no idea that they had adopted a pet. So as he was unaware, he dropped the newspaper at the usual place. So when grandma opened the door of the balcony, she gasped in complete shock. What actually happened was hilarious. Ronnie was hiding behind his chair and the whole balcony was filled with tiny pieces of the newspaper. No wonder it was done by him. Stephen and Penny were a bit angry at first but they laughed instead.

After all, it was pretty obvious that Ronnie felt guilty. So there was no need to be mad at him.

Ronnie was getting naughtier and naughtier day by day. No matter what, he was a part of the family. He filled everyone's heart with positivity and happiness. It was like a blessing. Every pet owner feels the same. Happiness was filled not only in the family but in the whole neighborhood. Mr. Snow and the kids used to take Ronnie for a walk regularly. Ronnie was like a third kid to Mr. and Mrs. Snow. And Kacy was the happiest of them all. At least that's what she felt. Even when Ronnie created a mess. They did get a bit mad at first but couldn't stay like that for longer. Ronnie was the newest member of Kacy's friend's group. All the kids loved to play with Ronnie. Grandma also got really close to Ronnie. Mrs. Snow loved to spend time with Ronnie while the kids were at school.

Mr. Snow felt like his life began when they got Ronnie. And no doubt, Ronnie was Peter and Kacy's new best friend... The First Experience for the family with Ronnie was bitter sweet. Mostly sweet... These Little Moments were the ones that made everything worthwhile.

CHAPTER FOUR

The Two Siblings

It had been 3 months after bringing Ronnie home. As mentioned earlier, dogs grow way faster than humans. That's why they are also fast learners. After 10 - 15 weeks of coming into this world, the training of a puppy starts. That means they're taught all the commands like sit, stay, eat, roll, shake hand, fetch, etc. when they are probably 3 - 4 months old.

"Fine, send me his number afterwards" said Mr. Snow hanging up a call.

"What did he say?" asked Mrs. Snow.

"They'll send us the phone number of the trainer." replied Mr. Snow.

Both of them were sitting on the balcony, having their morning tea, talking about finding a good trainer for Ronnie. The kids were at school. They didn't have any in their contacts so they decided to ask Mr. Cooper from Pet Spot.

In just a matter of time, Mr. Cooper sent the number of the trainer that he recommended to Mr. Snow. The trainer's name was Steve Russo. As soon as they got his number, Mr.

Snow dialled it up.

"Hello. Is this Steve Russo? The dog trainer?" he asked.

"Yeah. Who's this?

"My name is Stephen Snow. I got your number from Mr. Cooper. Just wanted to ask if you train Labrador puppies."

"Yeah I train all kinds of puppies. How old is yours?"

"He just finished 3 months, and I was wondering if he's old enough to start his training."

"Yeah he's of the perfect age. We can start his training right away if you want."

"Sure... when can you start?"

"I'll have to adjust my schedule a bit."

"Fine. Just give me a call afterwards."

"Okay."

After the call ended, they took Ronnie out for a walk. While they were on it, the trainer's call came and he told them when he'll be starting.

The next morning at 8 AM, the doorbell rang. Ronnie immediately started barking as soon as he heard the bell. Then Kacy went to open the door. When she saw through the peephole, there was a man in track pants and t-shirt standing there. It was the trainer. She had never seen him before so she called her dad to open the door. "It must be the trainer" saying this, he opened the door. "Come on in."

As soon as Mr. Russo entered, Ronnie went and started sniffing him because he had never seen him before. Then Mr. Russo took a seat while petting Ronnie. "What's his name?" he asked. "Ronnie." replied Mr. Snow. "He's quite energetic." said the trainer trying to get his keychain out of Ronnie's mouth. Then he shaked Ronnie a little bit checking his steadiness. He had a packet of treats in his left pocket for the training. It didn't take Ronnie much time to figure out about the treats as his smelling ability was pretty good for a 3 month old puppy. He sneaked over to the trainer's pocket to get the treats as they smelled delicious. But it took no longer for the trainer to figure out and pull Ronnie away from the treats. Because he would need them afterwards for the training.

While they were discussing the fees, Kacy got really excited as she had just found out that Ronnie was going to be trained. "Let's go to the ground to start the training." Mr. Snow said, attaching the leash to Ronnie's collar. "Dad, can I please come too, I also want to see Ronnie being trained." asked Kacy standing up from the chair. After dad said yes, Peter also joined them without asking because he knew if they didn't say no to Kacy, they wouldn't say no to him...

In just 2 months of training, Ronnie was able to sit, sleep, shake hands, roll, salute and do many more tricks on command. It's a bit unbelievable but Ronnie was halfway to his teenage years. Dog teenage years are between 8 - 12 months. Ronnie had gotten quite big...

After a few months, one sunny day when the trainer was on leave, Mr. Snow decided to take Ronnie for a walk. After some time, he decided to ride his bike in front of Ronnie to see how he would react. For some time Ronnie ran behind his bike but then who knows what happened to him, he ran in his full speed, and hit the bike. Due to which Mr. Snow lost his balance and the bike fell. He was quite surprised with Ronnie's strength. Because his bike wasn't a normal one, it was a big and heavy one which felt pretty impossible for Ronnie to even move it. Then Mr. Snow decided to check if Ronnie is able to jump from over it. So he parked the bike in such a way that it would block the other ways of going. Then he tied Ronnie's leash to one end and kept a treat on the other end with the bike blocking the way. Then he unleashed Ronnie. He wasn't able to jump over the bike in the first few times. But then, Ronnie figured out that the faster he runs, the easier it is to jump over the bike. Which he finally did. Mr. Snow was really surprised by what had just happened because the bike wasn't a small one.

One fine morning, mom and dad decided to go to "Pet Spot" to buy some stuff for Ronnie. They were youth of dog food and they also felt like Ronnie needed a new chew toy to play with. The kids were at school so they decided to take Ronnie with them.

Well Ronnie did like a sweet car ride. He loved looking at other cars and the cool soothing wind touching his face as the car moved. So yeah, he got pretty excited when he saw dad get the car out of the parking lot. He immediately ran and sat at the backseat with his head halfway outside the window and his tongue wobbling as the wind came.

Then after reaching there, Ronnie got really excited and started sniffing around as if he remembered the place. He was a month old the last time he was there so there was a 50 - 50 chance of him remembering the shop. Even if he didn't recall it, it was still a new place, so the excitement was as expected. Mom and dad tied Ronnie leash so that he doesn't create chaos in the shop. It was just a matter of time when other puppies in the shop started playing with Ronnie while mom and dad were busy buying stuff.

Mr. Cooper's brother was at the counter while Mr. and Mrs. Snow were shopping. After sometime, Mr. Cooper arrived at the shop as his shift had started. As soon as he saw Mr. and Mrs. Snow, he waved at them. Then they started talking...

When he looked at Ronnie while talking to Mr. and Mrs. Snow, he realised something really important he had been meaning to tell them. Something that was not so pleasant for a pet owner to hear. They were talking about the funny things Ronnie did. So he decided to wait for the end to tell them because he didn't want to ruin their mood.

"How is Ronnie's health? Is there anything unusual that you may have noticed about his eating habits, skin, barks or anything?" he asked.

"Not that we know of... he's been normal, we haven't seen anything unusual about his health. Why, what happened?" asked Mr. Snow.

"I don't know how to tell you this but... Do you remember the other 2 siblings of Ronnie? The ones which were here when you came here to get him?"

"Yeah, of course we do, the ones who were sleeping half of the time, right?" asked Mrs. Snow.

"Yeah, so they were adopted the very next day you guys took Ronnie. But last month itself we got a call from their owners, that both of 'em were affected by a disease related to skin and unfortunately both of them passed away one after the other with a gap of 2 weeks. In the first week, the female's owners' call came. And after 2 weeks the male's owners' call came. Since then we've been worrying about Ronnie."

"Ohh, how's that even possible? They were so young. I hope it's not a genetic problem." said Mr. Snow.

"The kids would be devastated if something happened to Ronnie. Let alone them, even we would be devastated." said Mrs. Snow.

"You should probably get Ronnie checked by the doctor." said Mr. Cooper.

"We should definitely do that. And if something comes up then we can directly start the medication." Mr. Snow added, looking at Ronnie with deep worry.

After getting the pet food and a new chew toy for Ronnie, they were ready to get back home. On the way they stopped at a vet to get Ronnie checked but then they decided to show him to Dr. Lang instead because he must be knowing more about Ronnie, as he's been vaccinating Ronnie from the start. The only thing they thought about while returning home was Ronnie. They were extremely worried.

After returning home and getting fresh, Mr. Snow immediately called Dr. Lang and received an appointment for the following day.

Then the kids came home. Mom and dad decided not to speak a word about Ronnie's siblings because they didn't want them to worry. Instead they gave them ice cream. While Kacy and Peter ate Cone Ice-cream, Ronnie was enjoying his vanilla flavoured one. It was his first time eating an ice cream. And it was adorable. The ice cream stuck on his nose and even though the cup was finished, Ronnie didn't stop licking it. It was a sweet treat.

The next day, Dr. Lang arrived at the house. He already knew what he had to check because Mr. Snow had already told him on the phone the other day.

"I thought the vaccination was already done last month" said Kacy in a confused tone.

Dr. Lang immediately realised that mom and dad hadn't told Kacy about that. "Yeah, but today I'm here for Ronnie's annual check up to see if Ronnie has some sickness or something else." he said.

Then he took Ronnie's blood to test it. And gave him some immunity medicines just in case. Now making Ronnie eat medicine was quite impossible. Vaccinating somehow felt more easier than tricking him into swallowing those really bitter pills. Sometimes they even tried melting the pills into his food. But of course the bitter taste didn't go away,which resulted into Ronnie not eating the food. The only thing that always works at last is holding Ronnie firmly and forcing him into swallowing the pill. Yeah that was tiring.

The blood test reports came the next day and Dr. Lang said that there's nothing unusual in Ronnie's reports. And that no sickness is detected. This gave mom and dad such a relief. They were so grateful that nothing came up. Then all the tension was gone. In fact they even went to the park after that. Eventually they thought that the other two siblings must have ate something poisonous which may have reacted with their health or that their owners were not able to take good care of them.

So everything was under control and everyone was happy. Ronnie was growing up and so was Kacy...

CHAPTER FIVE

Moving

"It also has a bathtub!!" Peter said while watching the video of their new home. Dad had taken the video when they went to see a new place to stay on rent while the original house was being built up. The kids were really excited because their new home was quite bigger than the quarters in which they were living and it was the first time they were moving to a different place.

It was the summer of 2014, the month of April. Kacy had just finished her 2nd grade and was ready to move to 3rd. Peter was still in kindergarten. It was quite amusing that Kacy's grandma was still working as a nurse in the hospital. If it wasn't for her, they wouldn't be staying in the quarters. It was the one thing that Kacy liked bragging about, having a grandma who's still not retired. Yeah she had one of those cool young grandmas. At least that's what she loved to think. But as years go by, people grow older. Grandma was 59 and it was finally time for her retirement. So they were ready to find a new home as they won't be living in the quarters anymore after grandma's retirement. Their plan was to stay on rent till their real house was being made. Luckily, they were able to find the rental house right in front of the working place where their house was being built.

"Mom, after moving, does it mean that I won't get to see my friends again? And please don't tell me that I have to change my school too." Kacy asked worryingly.

"No dear, your aunts still live here, so you'll get to meet your friends. Don't worry. And it's not that far that you are gonna have to change your school." Mom said consoling Kacy.

At first she was really worried when she thought that she wouldn't get to meet her friends again but when she realised it won't be that bad, she got really excited because it was the first time she was moving. She had been living in this house since she was born so this was new. But she was still a little bummed out because she won't get to play with her friends everyday as usual. So she decided to spend most of the time with them before they start packing.

In the evening, all the kids and Mr. Snow were playing with Ronnie on the ground. Ronnie was in his own excitement running all around the ground with Kacy and her friends. Then, one of Kacy'd friends, Ray decided to hold Ronnie from his collar for some reason. A second had barely passed and he was already being tossed around the whole ground. Good thing he didn't get hurt but was frightened for sure. It was such a funny senario that everyone just couldn't hold their laughter.

The next day, dad and Peter brought some cardboard boxes to start packing small stuff like the utensils and electronics. Those were just cardboards, they needed to be taped to turn them into boxes. Sounded like a job for Kacy because she loved doing that kind of stuff. Like arts and crafts was her thing. But mom and dad knew that they couldn't completely rely on her as she would probably take one whole day to finish taping all of the boxes.

So while grandma was at her retirement party at the hospital organised by her colleagues and her friends. Mom and Kacy were bonding over which tape to use to fix the boxes. And by bonding I mean arguing. It was just a matter of time when Ronnie started making a mess by taking the cardboards here and there. He was too big to fit in his bed so they eventually had to tie him to his leash. Because after the training started, they let him roam freely in the house as he had become pretty disciplined. Luckily, Kacy and mom were able to settle at duct tape finally after arguing for almost 15 minutes. Even though they worked for the entire day, a whole lot of packing was still left.

"Oh come on... we've barely moved anything." Kacy whined, wiping the sweat off her forehead. "How are we supposed to pack the whole house?"

"Have some patience. Nothing will work fine if you keep on complaining like this." scolded mom as she was tired herself and in no mood to hear Kacy's tantrums.

"What's this?" Kacy asked, holding a little jumpsuit in her hands. It was so small that it won't even fit Ronnie. It was of light blue colour with small ducklings on it.

"That's yours."

"I don't remember wearing it, ever."

"Of course you don't, we had brought this a couple weeks after you were born. You were so little." Dad said remembering the good old days.

This wasn't the only thing that they found. There were a lot of old stuffed toys and playsets too. Some of them were really unknown to Kacy but some just reminded her of some really sweet memories.

After a week of hard work, the packing was finally complete. It was Saturday and they were supposed to leave on Monday. So Kacy decided to invite all of her friends from the neighborhood just to have one last "party". Well, Kacy and her friends' definition of party was to just bring different kinds of snacks and watch a movie together. So she told dad to bring some chips packets and juice boxes for her and her friends.

Then all of her friends brought different kinds of snacks and chocolate which made it a complete treat.

Millie was really sad with the fact that Kacy was moving because she was her only best friend in the whole neighborhood.

"Here." said Millie, holding out a bracelet with half a heart on it. It said 'forever' on it. "This is something for you to remember me when you leave. I have the same one, it just says 'Best friends' on it." she added showing the bracelet she was wearing.

"Best friends forever... " said Kacy.

"Yeah, and don't you dare forget me. Even after you make new friends."

"Of course I won't. Plus, I'll have this bracelet which will keep me reminded of that."

This made both the friends really emotional but they decided to laugh it out instead as they didn't want their last memories to be emotional. Then all of the kids watched a cartoon movie together.

Moving day was finally here and family was ready to start moving. Dad brought some labourers to help in taking heavy furniture and electronics to the moving trucks. While Kacy and Peter were busy playing, the others were busy helping. It took them the whole day to empty the whole house. And the feeling of seeing their house empty brought goosebumps on everyone. Saying goodbye for the last time brought many flashbacks of the past. Too many memories were attached to the house. Some were sore and some were the sweetest of them all. It all felt so fast. They just didn't want to leave the house in which they spent most of their life in. Eventually, tears were shed and memories were recollected and it was time to say goodbye.

New house seemed nice but didn't feel like home as everything was new. The kids slept peacefully but mom, dad and grandma had some trouble falling asleep. It was either because the house was new or the fact that the air conditioner was still left to attach.

They left half of the stuff packed as it was just the rental house and they would have to move again because their new house was almost finished with all the work to be done. So they only unpacked the essentials.

Kacy and Peter loved the house. Because they didn't have a bathtub in their old home. So that was a new experience. They even made Ronnie bathe in it. It was really spacious so there was more space for Ronnie and the kids to play.

Luckily the neighbors were also kind. They didn't have any problem with Ronnie's barks. Except the house owners who didn't want a dog roaming in their house. But Mr. Snow somehow managed to talk them out of it.

It was a bit hard at first for Kacy to make new friends. The funny thing was that Ronnie had immediately made a new friend. His name was Tuffy. One day when Dad was out walking Ronnie in the new neighborhood, they found out that the neighbours also had a dog. It was a huge Labrador Retriever. And it was pretty visible that he was older than Ronnie as Ronnie was still a puppy. Both of them made really good friends. They did not fight at all. Instead they used to scare away the other stray dogs. Even the bigger ones. Tuffy's owners were the Duncans. They had a little son around Peter's age so Peter also instantly made a new friend. His name was Ricky. Poor Kacy was still left. But it didn't bother her at all. She still had school friends whom she was soon going to meet after the summer holidays ended.

This neighborhood was quite peaceful as there were really less vehicles compared to the quarters. The quarters were in the city so the horns were a great menace there. But here the peacefulness was so calming.

It took some time for the family to settle there. But eventually everything turned out perfectly. Kacy was finally in 3rd grade. Her school was a bit far but it was managed. In a couple of weeks Kacy also made some new friends and they started playing every evening. She got a little homesick at first but she eventually got over it. Grandma was loving her retirement. She now had a lot of free time to play with her grandchildren and even get along with Ronnie...

CHAPTER SIX

THE BITE

It was the winter of November. The sunlight was falling right on the balcony flaunting it's golden glow. It did bring a bit of warmth but the cool winter breeze flew it all away. Little sparrows were chirping on the tree waiting for their mom to bring in food. And the calming piano music was being played on the record player. Nothing could've been better. The perfect evening. The family was sitting in the balcony one last time in their rental home. With everything packed as the last time for their next and the final shift. Peter was playing video games in mom's phone and Kacy was busy playing with Ronnie. They were having a tug of war on one of Ronnie's chew toys.

The next day itself, they started moving to their new and final house. Good enough to be called home. This time the shifting was supposed to be a bit faster as their new house was right in front of the rental one. But what took the most of their time were the stairs. Their apartment was on the 2nd floor so moving the heavy couch, refrigerator, T.V., beds etc. was a bit of a hard deal. It took the whole day for the labourers to move everything in. But in the end it was all worth it. The new home looked really amazing, everyone loved it. And somehow it felt like home instantly.

"Finally!" Kacy said with a sigh, jumping and laying on the couch. "Well, this was tiring. But mom, dad, the house looks so amazing... I guess everyone's hard work paid off."

"Sure did... Now we don't have to worry about moving again." said dad.

"Yeah. Now those rental owners will also not trouble us by complaining about Ronnie." mom added.

"Exactly, they were so annoying. Plus, now we can do any variations we want. Maybe get some new wallpapers and carpets. We can also put some new show pieces." said grandma.

"Grandma, we just got here!" laughed Kacy.

Then they had dinner and went to bed early as it had been a very long day.

On the other hand, Ronnie's training was finally complete. It made playing with him much more fun. Not that it wasn't fun before. But this time his skills were really on another level. Dod used to hold Ronnie's leash till Kacy and Peter went to hide the treats at the different corners of the house. Then dad would release Ronnie and command "Search!" Then Ronnie goes sniffing around the house and within no time, he finds his treats. This was really amusing for everyone. Kacy just couldn't believe how he did that. Because first of all the treats didn't have a strong smell. And Ronnie would literally smell it from the other room and get it from any corner. Not only this, he also took the stay command seriously. Dad and the kids would show Ronnie his treat and then command him to stay. Then they would put one on his forehead, one on his back, even two on his legs. Ronnie was so good that he didn't even move a little bit. Even though those were his favorite treats. Probably because he knew that eventually dad would let him eat them. Yeah but he did drool. Like those drooling cartoons who get too excited on seeing their favourite food. And the look he gave while staying, was capable of melting the heart of anyone. He would look at us directly into our eyes so innocently that not even a tuff man would help but give him the command "Eat". It was pure emotional blackmail. Funny in some way, but it worked every single time.

Now that they had moved here, Tuffy's house was on the other side of a high wall. Tuffy was a really huge dog so there was no way he would have jumped off the wall. So dad taught Ronnie to do it. So that both the friends could meet each other everyday.

Flashback:

'Let's go back to October 2013 for a while... Ronnie was still a puppy. And it was a really new experience for both Kacy and Peter to grow up with a dog. No matter how cute and little Ronnie was, Peter was still scared of him as he had not played with such an energetic puppy before.

One afternoon in the beautiful season of fall, Peter suddenly got an urge to play with Ronnie and made him run behind him. At first, he started sliding his hand on Ronnie's forehead. This made Ronnie think that Peter wanted to play. And in just a matter of time, he started running behind him. And as expected, Peter freaked out. The began shouting and running here and there. And before they knew it, something started burning on Peter's ankle. Ronnie's intention was just to play but who knew, his teeth slit Peter's leg. It wasn't a deep cut. But it did bring out one little drop of blood. Peter didn't realize it until he finally looked at it. And when he did, he started crying. It was like he was crying because of the fact that he was bit and not because of pain. Or maybe he was crying because he was extremely worried about getting injections for rabies because when they brought Ronnie home, he heard mom and dad talking about the same.

That evening mom and dad took him to the doctor. He immediately suggested them to make Peter take the vaccine for rabies.

The very next day, Peter's dose of vaccination started. And he had to take a total of 14 injections, each one after a specific number of days. He was really really mad at Ronnie for that but they eventually got along...'

Anyways, now let's get back to the present...

"The sunset is so beautiful! Dad, let's go to the terrace." said Kacy while eating the cookies that grandma made. "We'll sit there till dinner is ready."

"Yeah dad, it'll be fun... Let's take Ronnie too." added Peter mumbling as he was still eating the cookies.

"But what do you wanna do on the terrace? I thought you guys wanted to watch that movie." said dad.

"No that's fine we'll watch it tomorrow!" said the siblings together.

"Alright, alright just lemme get fresh first and then we'll go. Okay?"

"Yes!" The kids jumped in joy.

Then they took Ronnie's leash out and went upstairs. Ronnie was just as excited as the kids. He immediately went upstairs leading it's way to the terrace before everyone else. Then they took the chairs out first to sit there and play ludo together on dad's phone.

After opening the door of the terrace, they did not see it at first but just in a moment, dad realised that there was a monkey sitting right at the corner of the railing. When the kids saw it, they for scared and took a few steps back. So dad decided to take Ronnie out thinking that the monkey would get scared and run away. When Ronnie saw the monkey, he got kind of excited as he had never seen one before. So he started running towards it. And just how he ran, the exact same way he took the steps back. Because when the giant monkey saw Ronnie coming towards him, instead of getting scared, he showed his teeth indicating anger. He looked deadly. So dad decided to take the kids and Ronnie back down stairs as he didn't want them to get hurt. Kacy will never forget that monkey's face. She was extremely scared by it but at the same time, a bit mad too as he was trying to threaten Ronnie. She and Peter were a bit bummed out at first but afterwards seeing that monkey, watching a movie felt like a much better idea... That day did bring some nightmares for Peter. Rest all was normal as usual.

The next day, mom, dad, Peter and Kacy were sitting in the balcony. Ronnie was eating his food, licking every single drop of the gravy as if it was the last time he was eating it. That was his daily routine. No matter how much of that dog food he got, it wasn't enough. Plus, the excitement he had while eating it was like no other. It was like everything around him disappeared as the food came. Even if he ate the same gravy everyday, he never seemed to be bored from it. Well, good for Mr. And Mrs. Snow. Now they don't have to worry about getting Ronnie's ideal food which he wouldn't just leave without eating.

Now let's get back to the point, so while they were chilling on the terrace, a call came on mom's phone. It was nona. She picked the phone from the table and went to the other end of the terrace because there was a lot of disturbance because of Kacy and Peter playing with dad. After finishing a talk of 25 minutes, which was not a surprise to anyone as her call with nona always lasted that long, mom came back to sit with the family. Dad could see the stress on mom's face for which he didn't know the reason to. He immediately asked her if everything was okay.

"Dad's not well. He got those convulsions again last night and only mom is there with him. He hasn't eaten since then." she replied hesitantly. "We'll probably have to go there because none of my sisters or brother is able to manage a leave. But I think that maybe we can."

"Sure dear we can leave tomorrow itself if his health is getting worse. Plus, we haven't been there for months so it'll be good." Dad said, comforting her.

Penny's parents (Kacy and Peter's grandparents) lived in a village far from any other city. They had started living after getting retired. Now matter how much their kids tried to convince them, they didn't want to leave the village (their home). Yeah unlike the cities, it wasn't developed with tech and everything, but the nature was too peaceful, with greenery everywhere, in the farms and mountains, the lake and wells were also filled with crystal clear water. And the place literally looked like a wallpaper.

The kids got really excited when they heard that they were going to go to their grandparent's house as they had not been there for almost 6 months. They started packing as soon as they got downstairs. They packed their pajamas and full sleeve t-shirts because there are a lot of mosquitoes at nana's house. So mosquito repellents were also kept. And everything was ready.

Then, while they were having dinner, suddenly a thought struck their mind. Where will they keep Ronnie? They can't take it to the village because they don't want him to get sick. They can't let him stay here because grandma cannot take care of him alone. Because Ronnie's force is really strong and it would be too much for grandma to handle. And they don't want to risk that. Because the last time they left Ronnie alone with grandma, the very next day they found out that she had tripped while walking him. And that was the time when Ronnie was still not fully grown. So now there was no better option than to send Ronnie to a pet day care or something like it. Mr. Snow tried calling his friends and relatives but everyone was busy. But a few call later, his eyes came upon "Mr. Russo" (The Trainer's) number in his contact list. He immediately called him, thinking he might have some solution. He didn't pick up at first so Dad thought that he might be busy training dogs. After all that's his job. Mr. Russo was the last hope to find a solution because or else they would have to stay at home and send Mrs. Snow alone.

A few minutes later, the phone rang on the desk. "It's the trainer." Kacy shouted, taking the phone to dad. He was actually relieved because he thought that the trainer's phone number was changed.

After greeting for a little bit, Mr. Snow got to the point, he said, "Mr. Russo, do you know any place where we can keep Ronnie for some days while we're gone. Because my father in law is really sick and we need to get there as soon as possible. And we are probably going to leave tomorrow morning."

"I do have a few dog day cares in mind but I don't think I would suggest them to you because I wasn't satisfied with their work. Ronnie is a disciplined dog so I guess it won't be a problem but they only take puppies for keeping."

"Ohh. Okay. By any chance, if you can find some place then please give me a call."

"You can keep him at my house if you want. Plus, Ronnie will be really happy to meet my dog too. My mom is really experienced in talking care of dogs so it won't be a problem while I'm at work."

"Are you sure you'll be okay with it?"

"Yeah of course! And Ronnie is familiar with me so he'll fit right away."

"Thank you so much Mr. Russo. You really took off a lot of stress. I'll send you the money for the food and other essentials right away. I hope Ronnie won't trouble you much."

This brought such relief for Mr. Snow. Now they could finally leave without a worry. He was really grateful to Mr. Russo. And having done that, everything was back in line. Their stuff was packed and they were ready to leave the following day.

The next morning, they were all set to leave. All the package was kept in the backside of the car. The kids took some board games for the road as it was a 3 hour ride.

"Where will we put Ronnie?" Mom shouted. "Why didn't we think of this before?"

"Did you not hear me talking to Mr. Russo last night?" laughed Dad. "We are gonna keep Ronnie at their house."

"Wait, is he okay with it?"

"Well, he was the one who came up with the idea so yeah."

This was a great moment of entertainment for the kids seeing that their mom was so absent minded that she didn't even know what was going on in her own house. After some time, they were off on their way to the trainer's house with Ronnie.

On the way, they decided to buy some ice cream for Ronnie before they leave him to the trainer's house. It was the kids idea. They stopped at a dairy store. The kids bought 2 cone ice creams for themselves and a cup one for Ronnie. They had to eat it there itself because they didn't want to make a mess at the trainer's house. Ronnie ate the ice cream happily and it was all over his mouth. After wiping it off they were ready to finally send Ronnie.

Then they reached the trainer's apartment. They tied Ronnie to his leash and went upstairs while dad was parking the car. The doormat had a bone printed on it in black with a white background. Under the bone it said, "Peace, Love and Muddy Paws..."

The saying showed the love Mr. Russo had for dogs. It didn't take much time for the barking to start as soon as the bell rang. It was kind of a high pitched bark, unlike Ronnie's, his was a deep bark which surrounded. In a few seconds, Mr. Russo's mom opened the door. She didn't seem surprised as she was expecting them to come as Mr. Russo had told her. He wasn't at home as he was at work.

"Hii, we're the Snows, is this Mr. Russo's house?" Mom asked holding Ronnie's leash. They kids looked at the woman with little fine lines on her face who looked like she was probably 48 or something. She had a really kind smile. It was a bit hard to believe that it was the trainer's mom. "Yeah, I'm his mom. And this must me Ronnie." she said, petting Ronnie. "I was waiting for y'all. Come on in. My son was just about to come home. He'll be here soon..." Saying this, she guided them inside the house.

"Thank you so much... I'm Penny Snow and these are my kids, Kacy and Peter." Penny said, slightly pointing at the kids.

Just as they got in, a really fluffy golden Pomeranian came out of the room barking, and started sniffing Ronnie. "And this is Goldie. Our silly little dog." said Mrs. Russo. "I'll bring some tea."

"No it's totally fin..."

"I wasn't asking." Mrs. Russo interrupted with a little smirk and went on her way to the kitchen. The kids chuckled.

Goldie went directly to Ronnie when she came out of the room. Both started sniffing each other. Then Kacy took her in her hands because she was really really excited as she had never played with a Pomeranian before. "Oh my God she literally looks like a pom-pom! Her fur is so soft! " she said in excitement. Then she handed her to mom. She reminded mom of their old dog which was a white Pomeranian which they had before Kacy was even born. Peter was also super excited while playing with her. But Ronnie and her seemed to have mood changes evey now and the like little teenagers. One second they were playing and the next thing you know, they are fighting over a toy.

A few minutes later, dad and Mr. Russo came. As they entered, both the dogs immediately ran towards them. Mr. Russo too was really happy after meeting Ronnie.

Then Mrs. Russo came with the tea which she made for everyone. And the moment when Goldie saw the tray in her hands she did something highly unusual. It wasn't unusual for the Russos but for the Snows, it definitely was. Goldie was jumping on her two back legs with the front two in the air along with really sharp barking. Mrs. Russo said that it was her way of asking for food. Which was quite impressive. The Snows had never seen a dog like this.

"Bye Ronnie!!" Kacy and Peter shouted while going down the stairs. Kacy didn't realize that at first but deep down inside she knew that she was gonna miss him. It was the first time she was going away from him. Before that she hadn't spent a single day away from him. So this was going to be hard.

After a ride of 2 and a half hours, they finally reached the village. The sun was setting behind the beautiful mountains. The farms were shining with green leafy veggies. And it was a view to be embraced. As soon as

Nana opened the door, she gasped in excitement. She didn't know they were going to come. So it was a huge surprise. Penny was also really happy after meeting her parents after almost half a year. Grandpa's health was a lot better now. It was so nice meeting them after such long time. The kids did have a lot of fun there but it would've been better if their cousins were also there. They stayed there for almost a week. It was refreshing but they didn't want to trouble the Russos for too long so they decided to come back.

When they reached the Russos' house, Kacy was the first one to run across the stairs to meet Ronnie. As soon as she saw him, she went and gave him a ginormous hug. Ronnie started licking her face excitedly. He had also missed Kacy a lot and got extremely excited when he saw her. Then mom, dad and Peter came and met with the Russos and Ronnie. Then Ronnie and the family finally got home...

Grandma was also glad that they came home soon because she was also missing them terribly. Theydecided to have dinner early and go to bed because they were exhausted after such long trip.

The next day, mom and dad were the first ones to wake up from Ronnie's barks as he needed to go for a walk. They somehow managed to get fresh before Ronnie did his business in the living room itself. Grandma and the kids were still asleep.

They were walking in the neighborhood just as usual holding Ronnie's leash, talking about some personal stuff and Ronnie was as usual in a mood of playing. Most of the time, Kacy and Peter also walked with dad and while they were at school,it was mostly mom and him both.

Suddenly, a sound of Ronnie's whine came. He reflexed back in force to the other side of the street. His force resulted in his leash getting loose and dad lost the hold of it. Then mom and dad saw a black stray dog come out from under the car they were walking beside. He was almost the size of Ronnie and was heading right towards him. Dad immediately took a rock and threw at him. Luckily, the stone didn't hit the black dog and it ran away. Everything happened in no time. It was so fast that no one had a clue about what had just happened.

They immediately went towards Ronnie to check if he was okay. He was bleeding from the bite of that stray dog. So dad immediately lifted him and they went back to the house. Ronnie was clearly in pain. He was barely letting anyone touch the wound. Still mom managed to apply some antiseptic cream on it somehow. They were lucky that the dog ran away immediately without reaching Ronnie from that car. Or he would've bitten him again. But he already did that from under that car. That was the reason Ronnie whined and ran with such a force.

Grandma, Kacy and Peter had woken up and were extremely shocked on seeing Ronnie in such pain. They had never seen Ronnie in that kind of situation before. They could see drops of blood spread on the floor. It was so little but felt too much. It wasn't bleeding that much but it was painful.

So mom and dad immediately took him to the hospital. They didn't even want to wait for the doctor's appointment. Luckily Dr. Lang was there, so he checked Ronnie. He gave him an injection to numb that part of the wound so that he could clean it thoroughly. Seeing Ronnie on that bed gave both the parents chills. But then finally it was all over. It didn't even take much time. Luckily Ronnie was okay and his health wasn't critical. "He is fine now and we're lucky that the bite wasn't too deep." Dr. Lang said.

"Thank you so much Dr. Lang."

"If anything comes up because of the medicine or anything, just give me a call." he added. "And I'll come next weekend to check on him. Till then it's nothing to worry about. And if there a lot of stray dogs in your neighborhood then you might just wanna carry a stick with yourself while taking him for a walk. Most of the dog owners suggest the same."

Then they left the hospital. Ronnie didn't seem to like the band aid but there was no other way to keep it away. from germs. After reaching home, dad immediately called animal control and scolded them on the phone complaining about how they are not regular in their neighborhood inspection. Kacy got really furious at that stray dog. Mom and dad were also really really mad. They were kinda grateful that the stray dog didn't come while the kids were playing. It took a few days for Ronnie to get used to the band aid but as soon as he got used to it, it was time to get rid of it. Dr. Lang came a week later and removed it himself. Ronnie was fully cured after that. This had been a really bad week for the family. It was full of stress and regret. Mom and dad took a lot of care while walking Ronnie from that day on...

CHAPTER SEVEN

THE DISEASE

"Go... fetch!" Peter shouted in his loudest voice possible as Ronnie swiftly ran towards his green rubber toy shaped like a ring. Except, it was a bit bigger than an actual ring. With little spikes on it. Mom and Dad were at the mall. And Peter was bored as Kacy was doing her homework. Grandma was trying some new recipes for the kids. Peter cannot take Ronnie downstairs to play by himself so he decided to unleash him in the house itself and play. He would not have been able to do it if mom and dad were home. Or he would've gotten into trouble. Luckily, grandma didn't scold him.

A few moments later, when Kacy saw him playing with Ronnie she couldn't help but keep her homework aside and start playing with them. "What about your homework?" Peter asked teasingly.

"Oh, I'll do it later. Not much is left." Kacy said like she didn't care about the home work. Then suddenly a thought struck in her mind and she said, "What about yours? I thought you were supposed to finish those addition sums." she teased back.

"You know mom makes me do my home work." Peter replied.

They played fetch for a couple of minutes. And suddenly Kacy got an idea. She held Ronnie's belt from his neck so that he couldn't run away. "Peter, go and put this toy there." She pointed to the other side of the house. "But..."

"Just do it I can't hold him much longer."

"Fine..." he said with a little scoff. Then he took the toy and placed it where Kacy told him to. "What now?"

"Now just say 'On your marks, get set, go!'"

Peter figured out what Kacy was doing and he shouted, "No I wanna do it, I also want to race with Ronnie."

"Well, it was my idea so I'll go first. Wait... show Ronnie his toy first." Then Peter waved the toy so that Ronnie would see it. And as soon as he saw it, he started getting more difficult to handle. "Now move out of the way or you'll get hurt." Kacy shouted. "Don't yell... Okay... On your marks... Get set... Go!!" he shouted back.

Then Kacy released Ronnie and tried to keep up with him while running. But eventually lost. Then Peter laughed and said "That was so cool! Now my turn." They played the same thing over and over again. And every time Ronnie got the toy first. So between the races, they even played tug of war. Yeah it was quite difficult to take a toy out of Ronnie's mouth. This eventually made Kacy realize that this was a great practice for the selection for sports day this year. Then she started going off about how the teachers were being partial during the selection in 2nd grade. But now she knew that 4th grade was going to be lit just because now she has Ronnie. Grown up Ronnie because in second grade he was a little puppy so...

They weren't supposed to say anything to mom and dad about the afternoon but eventually they told them the whole thing as it was an incredible fun. Mom and dad did nothing but laughed. Luckily, they didn't scold...

A few days later, grandma was teaching Kacy to see a pattern on a handkerchief. "And this goes through here... Do you get it now, dear?"

"Yeah grandma."

"Oh finally!" grandma said with a scoff. She had been going over the same thing for like half an hour to explain it to Kacy. "Now take this to the living room, I need to clean this up."

"Okay!"

Then Kacy went excitedly to the living room where Ronnie was sleeping with his leash tied up to its usual place. She was running without even looking around. Then she went to get the sewing kit so that she could get more colours of thread. In the same excitement, when she reached the living room, she tripped near a mattress which was placed on the floor. Perhaps she didn't fall completely, but because of the tripping, the sewing box fell off her hands and everything inside it just fell on the floor giving a patter sound. All the needles, threads and buttons were spread. And because of the thud, mom came rushing towards the living room shouting, "What happened?"

"Nothing!" Kacy shouted back.

Then, directly, on seeing everything spread on the floor, mom gasped in shock and said, "Kacy, what did you do? And what are you doing with the sewing kit?"

"Grandma taught me how to sew patterns on this handkerchief and I thought of using some more colours. Don't worry, I'll pick it up"

"It's fine dear, just go and check if there's anything near Ronnie."

"Okay..."

"Yeah, we don't want Ronnie to eat any of that tiny stuff."

Just out of curiosity, Kacy immediately asked, "What happens if he eats something from that?"

"He may probably get extremely sick which is really not good."

"Really?"

"Yeah!" saying this, she went back inside.

Kacy was really shocked on finding that out. Though it wasn't that big of a deal but Kacy seemed to exaggerate her understanding and thought that, on eating one of those buttons or needles, Ronnie might die. Well she was right about the needles. Just thinking about it for some time, Kacy started crying immediately without even realising that Ronnie was still there with her. She couldn't even imagine her life without him. But whenever she did, she cried. No one can blame her, she's just a 4th grader. Even a thought of that may terrify a kid. Luckily, she was able to get hold of herself. But then she directly went towards Ronnie and gave him a tight hug. He immediately woke up and started licking her. But it didn't bother her, instead, she just stayed there.

Well of course she was so worried, after all, Ronnie was the only friend she had. Not really,she had a lot of people she could call her "friend". Every single one which she has ever had somehow turned their back on her. And the friends she has currently, indirectly make her feel like she's not welcomed in their group. They make her feel left out. And sometimes they are even rude to her. Still she doesn't realise that she doesn't need them. But with Ronnie it's the whole opposite. She never feels left out with him. Has the best time and the best fun. And she knows that he's gonna be with her forever.

A few days later, it was bath time. Mom decided to clean Ronnie. Every time she turned on the tap, Ronnie went and tried to drink it. And didn't stay at one place. Making mom loose hold of him. This was the struggle of everytime. Every single time someone decided to clean him up, sometimes, he liked those bath times and sometimes, he could just do anything to get out of it. And after bathing, without getting dry, Ronnie would just get out of the bathroom and run all around the house. No matter how many times he slipped, he kept on running. Who knows what kind of excitement he got that time. He did that everytime. One time, just to catch Ronnie, mom tried going after him so that he doesn't get hurt. But instead, she herself slipped which caused her a minor backpain.

A few days went by and Kacy and Peter were, as usual, playing with Ronnie. And he got tired after some time. Kacy realised that he was and needed sleep. So she told Peter to stop playing so that Ronnie could fall asleep. Then they decided to watch T.V. instead. A few minutes later, mom came and asked, "Why is Ronnie asleep, he just woke up."

"I don't know mom, he looked tired so I thought he needed sleep so we stopped playing." Kacy replied.

"Well, now we'll have to wake him up again because I just brought his food."

"Okay... "saying this, Kacy took Ronnie's food bowl near him to lure him awake. Which did it's job as expected. Ronnie woke up and started eating. Kacy sat there till he finished eating so that she could take the bowl to mom so that she could wash it later. Ronnie almost finished the full bowl but left some of it. He never did that. Kacy tried to take it near his face still he was not eating it. She sat there for almost 5-10 minutes but Ronnie didn't seem to eat any of it. So Kacy took the bowl to mom and showed her. "Mom he's not eating it."

"Did you try showing him the bowl?"

"Yeah I did, so many times, but he just didn't seem interested. I guess we'll just have to buy some new kind of food for him."

"Guess so."

While they were having this conversation, suddenly Peter shouted from the living room, "Mom! Ronnie just threw up!"

On hearing this both of them just ran towards the living room. Ronnie was sitting at the corner behind where he threw up. It seemed like everything he ate just came out. And he was still looking exhausted. So immediately after cleaning up, mom called dad on the phone and told him about what happened. So he immediately came home. They decided to take him to the vet because he was looking really exhausted and sick.

When they reached there, the doctor immediately started checking Ronnie without any appointment, because he was looking really sick. He even took some x-rays as Mrs. Snow told him that some stuff from the sewing kit was dropped by the kids and it may have fallen near Ronnie.

"It's nothing severe, I did not detect any sickness, it's probably some sort of food poisoning. Nothing much. And about the sewing kit, if anything unsual was in his body or stomach, the x-ray machine would've detected it. So there's nothing to worry about. He'll be better in a day or two. Just give him this medicine so that his digestion gets better. It's not necessary but if he doesn't eat anything then just make him swallow this." The doctor said handing out the medicine to Mr. Snow.

"Okay, thank you so much, doctor." they said. It was a relief that it was nothing serious but looking at Ronnie gave them chills. Because they has never seen him so weak.

Then they reached home and informed everyone that everything was okay.

The next day itself, Ronnie started feeling better and energetic again and also started eating. What made him feel more better was that he even got play with one of his best friends besides the family, Matt. Obviously Matt is also family but they didn't get to meet everyday like the quarters here. But that problem was now solved as Aunt Beth and Matt were moving to the same apartment as them. Well they did use to come once a month here but now that they live here, they can meet almost everyday. The kids were also super excited...

CHAPTER EIGHT

HOSPITAL!!!

A few days went by... Mr. Snow and the kids were playing carrom in the living room after having dinner. Kacy, in her own excitement, was talking about how her Sports Day practices were going to start and how she was going to destroy her competitor in the race selection.

She was really confident this time because she knew that from now on, every time she'll take part in a race or a sports event, it was going to remind her of how she practiced with Ronnie. And that sweet memory will keep all of the mean things that anyone else will say to her to lower her confidence, away.

While they were busy playing, Ronnie was sitting st his usual place, scratching himself the whole time. When mom noticed at first, she didn't think anything was unusual but after a few minutes she realised that he was scratching himself continuously.

"Don't you think Ronnie's scratching himself since too long?" she asked dad.

"I didn't notice, it would probably be some mosquito or a bug."

A few moments later, he stopped doing that and fell asleep. And it was time to go to bed. So they stopped playing and kept the carrom board to it's place and went to bed. While Mr. Snow was turning the lights off in the living roomroom, he thought of checking if Ronnie has some allergy because he was scratching so much. Ronnie was asleep, so he gently turned him around to see the area he was scratching. He didn't know exactly where it was but the suddenly he saw some small red dots forming a circle on Ronnie's skin. It seemed like a rash. But since Ronnie scratched a lot, it was also bleeding a little bit between the dots. Dad didn't know if it was because of the scratching or the rashes. "Penny! Come here..." he said. "What happened?"

"Look here." he said, showing the rashes.

"Oh dear! It seems like a rash. That's why he was scratching a lot."

"Yeah. He must've stopped scratching after it started to burn."

"Wait, let me get the antiseptic cream." She went inside and brought the antiseptic cream and applied it on the rash. "Maybe we should take him to the vet tomorrow."

"No I'll call Dr. Lang instead. I don't think the people from the vet checked correctly."

"Okay but do it soon."

"Yeah I'll do it, first thing tomorrow."

The next morning Dr. Lang came. He check Ronnie thoroughly and asked about his diet and routine or anything else. "It's some sort of skin disease, I mean it's not a simple rash. But in my years of training I haven't seen or even heard about this kind of disease. It's better if we start taking care of it right away. Because it looks a bit dangerous." he said. Then he took a photo of the rash area. "I'll show this to my fellow doctors but if it's some new kind of disease then we'll have to treat it like we treat other diseases. Right now,at the moment I have this antiseptic. But you can come to my hospital tomorrow morning, I'll keep the more effective one ready."

"Okay doctor. Is it that serious? I mean is there something to worry about?" Mr. Snow asked.

"Yeah, I mean, right now it's not that serious but if we don't take care then it'll be really hard to take care."

"Okay and how many times do we have to appy this antiseptic." Mrs. Snow asked.

"Apply this one for today but then apply the one I give tomorrow. That one is special for such kinds of diseases. This is just an antiseptic. And don't make him eat any spicy food. It will increase the rashes."

"Okay doctor."

Then Dr. Lang left. And Mrs. Snow applied the antiseptic on Ronnie's rashes. It seemed to burn a little bit but there was no other way. She tried to appy it softly so that it doesn't hurt that much. And for Ronnie's daily walk, they took him just to the back side of their neighborhood where it was cleaner. Because in dusty areas there's a lot of chance for the infection to spread. The rash was getting healed so they were able to sleep peacefully.

The next morning, dad got ready to go to Dr. Lang's to get the antiseptic. Before leaving, they decided to check the rash. While they were moving him, Ronnie gave out a little whine as he was hurting. They saw that there was a little circle where the it was bleeding a bit. It was near his stomach, near his back legs. The skin was bruised as if something was used to slit it. But last night when they saw, nothing was there. The skin was peeling. Dad decided to take a photo and show it to Dr. Lang while getting the antiseptic cream.

The doctor had no words. He himself couldn't make out what it was and how it was happening. He just said to keep giving the medicines and applying the antiseptic creams. And to make him eat cool food which would get rid of the heat which could've been the cause of the rashes. This was really stressful for the whole family. And the fact that even the doctor didn't what was happening was more terrifying.

No matter how much care they took, applied the creams, made Ronnie eat the medicines. Nothing seemed to work. Those were doing nothing but causing pain. The bleedig didn't stop,instead it seemed to get bigger.

Few days later, the rashes started increasing severely. Two new ones had come up. Luckily they were a bit smaller than the ones which were already there. But they looked the same. Redness was the same. And it hurt the same.

Sometimes mom and dad would just sit with Ronnie to make him feel better. The kids would also sit and make him play a bit. Ronnie also liked it. They tried to make him play fetch with his ring toy but he also lost interest in it. He wasn't able to run, he wasn't able climb walls as before. Well he was able to move and luckily the smaller wounds weren't growing like that big one near his leg. No matter how much it pained, he still got so much excited whenever they were about to take him for a walk.

Few weeks went by and that big wound started bleeding. It had turned a little white because of infection and clearly Ronnie was in a lot of pain. More than before. His cries made everyone feel terrible. Sometimes, Mr. and Mrs. Snow even started tearing up seeing Ronnie that way. They just didn't know why it was happening. Ronnie should be playing in the sun right now and here he his with this unrecognizable disease. He's just two years old.

Two agonizing months went by. With the same routine. Giving him sponge baths, checking if there is no dirt or houseflies near him, applying antiseptics, using some natural remedies, making sure that he's alright and dressing the wounds. Still his health was the same. It may have gotten worse but it didn't become any better. Everything was the opposite of what it used to be a few months ago. Kacy missed playing with him so much. She would cry and ask mom and dad when Ronnie was gonna get better. They used to reply, "Don't worry dear, he'll get better." even though they weren't sure. They didn't want Kacy to keep stressing about it. Because when they had recently moved from the quarters, Kacy was okay at first but then she had started getting homesick. Her blood pressure would get real low. And they would have to go and pick her up from school every time she had a headache. It started with homesickness but then she was just sick. Her headaches were some little symptoms of migraine. But with a few weeks of medicines, she was cured.

Ronnie barely touched his food now. Mom had to feed it to him. Still he used to eat very less. He couldn't sleep on his usual side because of the big rash. Ronnie had gotten thinner because of not eating much. Kacy and dad tried their best to cheer him up but he found it really hard to get up. He even stopped going for his favorite long walks. The ones for which he used to get so excited for. He had also become really pale and weak. Poor Ronnie didn't kow what was going in with him. He would try his best to just go and play fetch with the kids or do various new stunts with dad, take grandma's newspapers or go sit in mom's lap.

The very next day, mom and dad were discussing something in their room. Nothing was coming on the T.V. and Kacy was bored so she just roamed around the house.

Sometimes she would go to the balcony and look outside, then go to Ronnie and cheer him up a little. She could've done anything to cure him and make as energetic as he was before. And she wanted nothing more than to just get him back up and play like never before. She was just waiting for him to get up and be good and healthy again.

Then Mom and Dad called her. "Kacy!" They called. "Come here dear."

"Your mom and I were discussing about Ronnie." Dad said.

"Yeah I thought so. What happened?"

"We are thinking of taking Ronnie to a hospital and getting him admitted. So the doctors could check him correctly."

"And... when will he come back?" Kacy asked with her voice cracking a bit. She was trying her hardest not to start crying.

"After he's cured. Don't worry. Plus, it'll be good for Ronnie. You're seeing how much he's suffering right now. We'll get him back as soon as we find out he's cured. Because we cannot cure him here. Right?"

"You're right... But can we at least go and meet him every now and then?"

"Yeah sure. He'll love that too"

"Okay... " she said with a sigh. Then she went to the other room and stood in front of the mirror. She knew that Ronnie was gonna come back later all healthy and energetic again still she started crying for some reason. She herself didn't know what was going on and why it was happening. She knew in her heart that Ronnie was strong enough to defeat a silly disease. She had never talked to herself before but today something happened that she told herself in the mirror, 'Don't worry, Ronnie's gonna come back in a few days. He's gonna okay and better than ever. What am I tripping for? Everything's gonna work out exactly the way it's supposed to... ' saying this, she wiped up her tears and smiled at mirror and went to the living room. A few minutes later, Dad's friend, Uncle Ben came home. He sat in the living room for some time with dad and they were discussing something. Kacy couldn't hear anything about it because she and Peter were busy playing with Ronnie. So she didn't know what they were talking about. She told Peter about send Ronnie to the hospital.

A few moments later, they started packing up some of Ronnie's stuff. Kacy knew that they were going to take Ronnie but she didn't know that they were going to take him today itself. It was a complete shock. She went and hugged Ronnie before dad and uncle Ben took took. "Don't worry, the doctors will cure you in just a few days and then we can go and get your favourite ice cream. I'll wait for you. Don't get scared because it's a new place, they're all your friends who will get you back up. Then we'll play every single thing that we havent been able to play in the last couple months. And don't you worry because we'll be waiting for you right here, mom, dad, grandma, Peter and I. We'll come running as soon as we get the call that you have finelly defeated the stupid disease. I'll make sure that I bring mom and dad to meet you every now and then. And i will terribly miss you so please get well soon and please be strong. Just think about how we will play after you get well and how we'll go on our long walks. And remember I love you more than anyone and I always will."

Mom packed some of Ronnie's stuff. Then they woke him up and took his leash out. They pulled his belt gently so that he could get up. Well, he did get up but then sat again immediately. Then they tried to make him walk but he barely got up. They pulled his leash and he tried to get up and start walking, but he tripped. He was trying his hardest to walk, but he couldn't even make it past the main door. So dad decided to lift him up. Because there was no way Ronnie could've been able to walk off the stairs from the second floor. That was a long way. So dad had to lift him up, no matter how heavy he was. Then gently kept in the backseat of the car. Ronnie didn't even stick his head out of the window this time. He just laid quietly in the backseat. Didn't know what was happening. Didn't know where he was going. Couldn't focus on anything while in pain. Mom, grandma, Peter and Kacy were watching them go from the balcony. Halfway, then in no time they were gone... Already missing him and terrified of the way he couldn't even walk.

They had just left, and still the family could feel the emptiness in the house and in their hearts. Kacy didn't know what she was going to do the whole time till Ronnie came back. She just wished that the doctors at the hospital would say that Ronnie does not need to be admitted. He will get better at home itself. But that was clearly impossible. They sat there and waited for a call from dad saying that the doctors have found the cure and will cure Ronnie in just a week. Unfortunatey no call came.

Dad came back in the evening. Kacy rushed to the balcony as soon as she heard him come, hoping he brought Ronnie back. She asked with little sparkle in her eyes, with so much hope, "Did you bring Ronnie?" Even though she knew he didn't being him. Dad gently answered, "I told you dear, they will admit him. He was suffering a lot." "Yeah, I forgot." she said holding back the tears.

After some time, she became normal. Ronnie was going to come back so there was nothing to worry about. After all, he would be treated in a better way if the doctors took care of him for some time...

"God, I'm so sorry I've never prayed before bed. But I'm starting to do that now. I promise I won't miss a single day. Thank you so much for giving me this life. Thank you for giving me this lovely family. And my most thanks to you for bringing Ronnie in my life. He is really sick right now and in a lot of pain. I don't like to see him suffer. I'm so sorry if I did something wrong these years or something that would hurt someone. But I'm asking you for nothing but to please give Ronnie strength to get back up as he was before. I promise to always be a good girl from now on. I will pray every single night from now on. And once again thank you..."

CHAPTER NINE

FOURTH GRADE SPORTS DAY

Kacy started praying every single night from that day. She found it a bit difficult as she was new to that. But that was her only hope. The only thing she could do from her side was to not lose hope and to be positive. It was really hard not to pay attention to the emptiness in the house. Everything seemed really really boring. Everyone missed Ronnie terribly.

Somehow the week went by, and Kacy got impatient about asking when Ronnie was going to come back home. Not that she hadn't asked the same thing the whole week. "Dad, how is Ronnie? Did the doctors call?"

"No, they said that they'll call after Ronnie's cured."

"It's been a week so can we atleast go and check up on him?"

"No, I saw the hospital, they told us that there will not be any visiting hours as everyone around there is really busy."

"But that's not fair... The owners should have the right to meet their dogs. They can't just keep them away from them."

"It is what it is. You see dear, every hospital has their own rules. There's nothing we can do."

"Okay... " she said in her low voice.

Peter was little so he didn't ask many questions. He barely knew what was going on. Kacy was really mad at that stray dog who bit Ronnie a few months ago. Sometimes she thought that it was because of that bite that Ronnie got the skin disease. She was even mad at the cruel doctors of that hospital who didn't even care about the feelings of the dog's owners. But there was nothing she could do...

She didn't ask mom and dad every single day because she thought that they would get mad. And that they were also as lost as how Kacy was. She thought that it was a mistake to send Ronnie to that hospital. There sure would've been some more better ones.

So she didn't ask every day but as weeks passed, her curiosity got more and more. She knew that mom and dad were missing Ronnie just as much as she did. And maybe more because half of the time she was at school and mom and dad probably had spent more time with him. Plus, he was like a third kid to them. But she was also missing her best friend. The only reason she got excited for the school to get over was because she would get to meet Ronnie but now, there was nothing to look forward to. The only thing that kept her busy from thinking about Ronnie were the Sport's Day practices and nothing else. She cried herself to sleep every night thinking about how such terrible thing could happen to such a precious little being. It was so not normal for a 7-8 year old to cry herself to sleep everynight.

A few days later, the race selection came. She was realy really nervous. She had thought that the race was going to be a sprint but the P.T. teacher was told to make it an obstacle race. So for her class, it was 'Sack race'. In Sack

Race the competitors basically stand in sacks and jump forward till the finishing finishing line. It was a surprise to her also thay she got selected. Because she had only practiced once for it. It was really exciting because in the primary section of her school, they had Annual Day's and Sports days in alternate years. She was really excited to tell Ronnie about that even though he would not understand a single word.

A few weeks turned into a month still there was no word from the hospital. Kacy kept on asking Mom and Dad. The answer was the same. Sometimes they even scolded her for asking so much. Still she didn't lose hope. She was lost and confused and angry because she couldn't figure out what was going on.

It was finally sports day and she was extremely nervous and excited at the same time. She woke up at 5:30 AM. which was pretty surprising because mom always had trouble waking her up. But as it was Sports day, it was quite obvious. Mr. and Mrs. Snow were really happy to see Kacy in such excitement but they were also afraid to see her face if she lost.

The sports day started... The children performed the mass drill. And after everything, it was time for the races. First the first grade, then second and so on... While waiting at the back, Kacy was talking to her friends. One of her good friends, Frankie, was talking to Kacy about Ronnie. She told her how it all happened and everything. Then instinctively, Kacy told Frankie that her parents were going to take her to meet Ronnie if she won the race. She herself didn't know why she said that. Because it was a complete no from mom and dad to go and meet Ronnie. But still she hoped for it. She thought that she would be able tp convince them.

Then came the fourth grade's turn. Her heart started beating as fast as it could go. Then the coach shouted, "On Your Marks... Get Set... Go..." And all the eight competitors including Kacy started jumping forward. All of them giving their best. As they reached the finishing line, the judges caught 3 girls, 1st, 2nd and 3rd respectively.

And Kacy won! She came first. She just couldn't believe it. It was her first ever medal and it was a gold one. This was one of the best moments of her life. Her class teacher was praising her along with the whole audience and all of her classmates. She had never felt so confident about herself before. It was such a wonderful moment.

"Wow Kacy! Now you'll get to meet Ronnie. I'm so happy for you. Congratulations!" praised Frankie.

"Thank you so much!" Kacy replied.

"Can I see your medal? I've never won one so I really wanna see it."

"Sure."

After the sports day got over, Kacy ran towards mom and dad. They were so happy and proud. Dad immediately gave her a tight hug and congratulated her. Then, after meeting a few teachers and clicking a few photographs, they were ready to go home. Kacy's happiness was indescribable. She held her medal in her hands the whole way home. Then immediately after reaching home, she rudhed towards grandma and showed her medal. "Grandma I won!" Grandma was extremely proud of Kacy and just as happy as she was. Today was amazing. Probably one of the best days.

At night, all of the memories she had with Ronnie came in the form of flashbacks to her. And she cried herself to sleep. She was missing Ronnie so much. She didn't even know how he must be feeling. She just hoped that he didn't feel betrayed. Her crying was so intense that night, she couldn't even breathe. She remembered how she dreamed of wining a race while running with Ronnie.

A few more weeks later, they were having breakfast together. And Kacy was furious at mom and dad for not telling her anything. It had been 2 months. She asked the same question.

"When will Ronnie come back? Two months have passed. He must be feeling so lonely dad. Please at least give a call to the hospital."

"Kacy, the hospital people made us sign a contract." said mom. "The contract said that, you were not able to take care of the pet and his health. And if you want him to be admitted in our hospital, signing this contract, the pet will officially be ours. And cannot be taken back."

"That is so not true. Why would some hospital do that? He was our family. They can't just take that away from us. We sent him to get cured. Not to get adopted by some complete strangers. And if you knew what was happening then how could you even sign such contract."

"Kacy there was nothing we could've done. Would you have liked if Ronnie lost his life in front of you?"

"No, of course not."

"That was the only way for him to get cured and nothing else. Or he would've gone in a week or two. He wasn't even able to walk, the day we took him."

"So are you saying, I won't get to meet him ever again."

"No we're not saying that. We'll adopt a new one who looks exactly like him."

As soon as she heard that, she started crying without even waiting for a second. "Is this all a joke to you mom and dad? You're unbelievable!" She immediately rushed out of the room swiftly. Mom and dad had never seen her so mad at them. Kacy went to the living room, stilll crying. Her parents didn't try to convince her. Because they knew that it would only make it worse. They wanted her to face the reality. Whatever they said to seemed really impossible to Kacy but still was just a 9 year old. But her life had turned upside down. There was a part of her didn't believe what mom and dad said at all. There was also a part of her who wanted to believe it. But most importantly, there was a part of her who just wanted to know the truth and get rid of the whole confusion and wanted every single thing to get back like how it was before. But she had no other option than to believe that the hospital people kept Ronnie with them. Another night went with the breakdowns. Cried herself to sleep again. Didn't have a single clue what was going on. Poor little confused Kacy.

Weeks turned into months. She was sick of hearing the same made up reasons from mom and dad. Whatever it was, she didn't stop hoping to get Ronnie back one day. Prayed every single night without fail. Tried her best not to start crying every night. But sometimes she did. She had a couple of breakdowns every month. She was just a confused little girl who didn't know what was going on in her own life. It was really really hard to keep going without knowing the complete truth. Life was a mess. She somehow learned to go through it, or did she? She was still figuring that out herself. Sitting in the living room where Ronnie used to be everyday, reminded of him every single moment. The littlest of the things he did.

Months turned into years. Still the praying and hoping didn't stop. She had started to think that praying wasn't going to do anything but she had no option. That was what kept her going. As she got older, she tried to find little things that belonged to Ronnie, to keep as a memory. When mom and dad weren't at home, she would just go to their room and look in their documents and papers hoping she would find something related to Ronnie. She remembered that when they adopted him, they gave them the identity card or something like that. Which had Ronnie's name and breed and birthdate and every other information about him. But she didn't find anything. When she asked mom for it. She couldn't find it either.

Kacy came in sixth grade. Got a bit mature. She realised that it had been 2 years since the scenario. But she still wasn't able to let go. It was a really big deal for her. She missed Ronnie. Even though it had been two years and some memories were fading away. What else can you expect from a 10 year old?

In sixth grade, she finally had a sprint race in her middle school. Where she got two gold medals, the first student in her class to get 2 medals on the same day. Plus they were gold. So it was a pretty big deal. Every now and then when she looked at those medals she remembered how she used to force Ronnie to run with her. It brought a giggle every now nad then but also some really intense feelings. The crying got a little less. Too little to be even noticed. Sometimes when she talked to mom and dad about the memories. And the disease thing came up, she would start crying sometimes. The parents alsogot emotional every now and then.

When she came in 7th grade. Her school had divided the students into 4 houses for the team activities. Red, blue, yellow and green house. She was in the Red house. The inter house activities made where fall in love with sports more because of the teamwork. And luckily her house used to win every single years since she came in middle school. Just because she was so good at sports and studies too, she was able to make a lot of senior friends too. With was a good thing because her friends from her own class were a bit rude because of her achievements. But some friends were genuinely happy for her.

So anyway, in seventh grade, she had an Essay Writing Competition. The red house had been given two topics to write an essay about. "My Favourite Book" Or "One of the Best Days of My Life." She thought that the second opinion was a bit interesting. She wrote about the day Ronnie came in her life. And every single thing that happened since then. For the end she wrote that Ronnie passed away from old age. So that the judges don't get as confused as she is.

A few days later at school, Kacy's class teacher Mrs. Annie called her at her table. She asked her about the essay. About Ronnie. It was quite a surprise to Kacy that Mrs. Annie was interested in Ronnie. So she told ma'am the whole thing. Then she said that she also has a pet dog of the breed Beagle. And that she has also lost on of her pets before. She explained Kacy that a pet's life is not that long. Most importantly a dogs life. It maximum 10-15 years. Kacy felt really nice after talking to Mrs. Annie. She had never bonded with any of her teachers for something personal. Except yeah with her P.T. teacher, she was quite close because she was a mentor for Kacy.

A few days later, the principal announced the final results of the Essay Competition. Surprisingly Kacy got the second prize. She was really shocked because she had never got a certificate for writing before. And also because she didn't think she was gonna win the competition when she was writing the essay. She quite proud of herself for that.

This year her medal count turned to 5, she was in disbelief herself. 3 gold medals and 2 silver ones. And not only for the races but also for long jump. Due to with she was also awarded as the Best Athlete of her Middle School. This made her a lot more confident about herself. Before that she was a bit shy and insecure but the trophy gave her a whole another level of encouragement. Also made her parents and family proud. But the more closer she got to sports, the more curious she got about finding out about Ronnie. Four years had passed still she wasn't able to let him go. Every time the sports days came,she would recall how she told Frankie that her parents were gonna take to meet Ronnie once she won. She was also regretting that she never got to celebrate this little victories which felt like the most important, with Ronnie. Another trophy came the next year but a chance to meet him never came. She herself didn't know why she wasn't able to let go. She barely remembered much about him. And four-five years is a really really long time. It was really hard to just ignore the fact that he must still be somewhere right now. "He must be feeling so betrayed that his own family abandoned him. And there would not be anyone who could tell him that they didn't. And that there would not be anyone who could tell him that they still love him more than anything.

The eight grade was about to end. They were cleaning the house fully as they did every year. And something really really, unexpected came in the hands of Kacy. It was Ronnie's last chain which they brought. All these years she thought that she didn't have anything but photos to remember him by. And now she finds this. It was extremely unexpected but pleasant. Then came the usual tears. The same day she found an old phone of mom's. The one which she used when they used to live in the quarters. She was looking at the old photos. It brought the sweet old memories back. She had a lot of photo of Ronnie but she had never seen any videos. But tonight she found a really old video of Ronnie. Probably one of the firsts. He was so little. They were playing with him. Peter was running away. She and dad were teasing him with his toys. Mom was probably the one capturing the video. Grandma had found her place ona chair so that Ronnie could not reach there. Then he peed on the floor and she immediately went inside to get the mop to show mom and dad that's she is responsible. On seeing this video, she didn't know whether to laugh or cry. It was a bit of both. But she was really grateful for finding that... Because she didn't remember much about it and these refreshed all of those bittersweet memories...

Everything was not the same as it was before. There was no one to steal grandma's newspapers or scare Peter, do stunts with dad, trouble mom by running all around the house. There was no one to give those sweet long hugs to Kacy. No one to play fetch, no one to go for long walks with, no one to bark at every single salesman or dilivery man, no one to love the as purely as Ronnie did. All that was left was emptiness...

CHAPTER TEN

THE TRUTH

2020, the year when all the lives were changed. The whole world went into lockdown. People started working from home, kids had to attend classes on a phone, tablet, laptop or a computer. This is the year when Covid-19 virus entered our lives. People could not go outside their houses without wearing masks or having a little sanitizer bottle in their pockets. Social distancing became a necessity and everyone's life had turned upside down...

It was March, 2020. Kacy was kind of relieved that her exams had got cancelled because of the pandemic. But she was also a bit sad because she had prepared the whole syllabus. They were just chilling in the living room, watching a movie when the message came from the school. They had been informed that there won't be any classes till the government's orders. It didn't take too long for the school to send the exam cancellation circular too. So the summer vacation had already started. In short, a longer vacation. But as the pandemic started increasing. Everyone got really scared and took double care. Like washing the groceries after coming from the store. Cleaning themselves immediately after coming home from outside and you know, the basic pandemic rules.

Kacy and Peter had finally settled on the discussion of adopting a new dog. It took Kacy a lot of thinking to come to this decision. But still deep down inside she felt that, it would mean that she's betraying Ronnie. She was exhausted from getting the same answer every single time she asked about him. The worst part was that she didn't even know the name of the hospital where he was admitted. So she would have searched it up on Google. Just to see where Ronnie must be spending his days. Hopefully cured from the skin disease. She had no clue if he survived the disease or not. If he was still out there somewhere hopefully around nice people. Hopefully happy. And hopefully not feeling betrayed and not missing them because she knew how it felt. It felt like hell.

She always seemed to get tears in her eyes every single time she saw a video of pets having fun with their owners. Or the videos in which somehow, some Labradors resembled the exact face of Ronnie. Which happened fifty percent of the time as there's not that much difference between the dogs of the same breeds. One day she thought of searching about the disease that Ronnie had. She searched, 'Skin diseases in Labradors'. For which she got a surprising answer. She read several articles related to the topic. And almost all of them proved that that disease could be cured if taken full medical care. This made her so curious about what may have happened. She just couldn't help the urge to ask mom and dad about the same. But she always hesitated on asking them as they also got really sad after thinking about it.

The very next day, Kacy and Peter went to Mom and Dad's room for breakfast. They were having their usual talks. One led to another. And it finally reached the most important topic. She took up some courage and said.

"You know, I searched about the skin disease in Labradors yesterday. And you won't believe it, but all the articles suggested that it could be cured. What if Ronnie's still out there, dad? What if they cured him?"

"Kacy, we have had this conversation like a hundred times. And I am tired of having to tell you the same thing again and again." Mom said.

"Doesn't it bother you that Ronnie must still be out there? Feeling nothing but betrayed from the only family he ever had? How do you even know if he's cured or not? And I don't believe... I don't believe it for a single second that the hospital didn't call to inform about anything."

"Kacy, we're not having this conversation right now. Okay, so stop it." Dad scolded.

"Hmm." Kacy said while holding back her tears.

A few seconds later...

"You know what, I'll tell you but we never speak of this again. I don't want you to ask me or remind me of this again." Dad said.

"Hmm. I won't only if you tell me the truth because I don't believe the contract thing at all."

"You do remember how he barely got up, on the day Ben and I took him, right? He was hurting even when I lifted him. When I put him in the backseat he was having trouble sitting because the rash was bleeding. So Ben had to drive and I sat behind to keep Ronnie from tumbling over. It took us an hour to reach there as we were going slowy. We tried to encourage Ronnie to get out of the car by himself. But he couldn't. So I had to carry him as before and took him inside. Then we had to wait for the doctor to finally come. Then he checked him and said "His health is really critical. Do you have any kids at home?" For which I replied, "Yes." Then he said, "Still you kept him at your home? This disease is really severe and I recall, on phone you told me that his siblings died two years ago. You all were lucky that nothing happened to him earlier, you might have taken really great care of him. And I don't know how to tell you this but this disease is genetic and not much can be done. So curing of this is quite impossible. Because I even checked him but still its not convenwd to even start any treatment. And he's at the last stage of this disease so I don't think he'll make it for even 2 weeks. And there's nothing we can do about it. If we let him be, and you take him home right now, then he's going to die a very painful death eventualy. And, it will be in front of your family and kids. It would be painful for him as well as your family. So in my opinion, the best option here is to euthanize Ronnie. It will not cause any pain. And he'll be put to sleep peacefully. Now it's up to you to decide."

When he said this I froze. I didn't know what to do or what to think for that matter. It was breaking my heart to see Ronnie in such pain because of the disease and I couldn't have been able to handle seeing him die painfully in front of our eyes. So after some time of thinking carefully, I asked, "What will happen if we try to send him to a forever sleep? Will he feel it? What's the process exactly?"

Then he expainwd the whole thing to me, "Euthanasia is a controversial issue and has many definitions but when it comes to our pets it literally means a quiet, gentle and painless way of dying... The procedure itself is very quick and gentle and the pet simply falls asleep. He will be given a concentrated overdose of the anaesthetic so that he peacefully falls asleep and then passes away. I will inject the euthanasia solution into Ronnie's vein, where it'll rapidly travel throughout the body. Within seconds, he will become unconscious, experiencing no pain or suffering. Breathing will slow down and then stop over the next several seconds. Cardiac arrest will soon follow, resulting in death. He'll feel nothing. He'll just fall asleep as he usually does and then within a few seconds he'll be gone. So do you want to do it?" And I said yes. There was no better option. He was already in pain and I don't think we could've been able to see him in more.

Then I hugged Ronnie, said a few words to him to make him feel comfortable, he was right there in my arms, looking at me as if he was thinking "Stephen will take me home after all this and I'll meet my family again." He didn't have a clue what was going to happen to him.

Then the doctor put him on the table and tied him up and started giving the first dose. I couldn't handle seeing it, so I immediately went outside of the room. And then the doctor came outside and said that the procedure is done and Ronnie is finally put to sleep.

You can ask your uncle Ben if you want to. He'll tell you the same. It was really hard to let him go... you thought that I would just leave him in someone else's hands for so long and not even give a call to them. But I was hurting more han you were Kacy.

And everytime you asked me about it, I didn't tell you the truth because I didn't want you to feel how I was feeling. And you were already sick because of moving from the old house. I lost one kid already and I was not ready to see you in pain either."

The whole time when dad was saying this, he was crying, mom was crying and even Peter had started crying. And Kacy had already started tearing up when she heard the word euthanasia. She didn't know what to say. Her mind was still processing the fact that Ronnie was gone on the exact day she last met him. And the way dad described the whole thing, it couldn't have gone worse. Her tears just weren't stopping. And in a really low voice she asked, "Why didn't you tell me this before. I asked you so many times." She had a lot of cracks in her voice because of crying and also because she couldn't even breathe because of excessive crying. Then mom added, "And it was a genetic problem. We were lucky that he even survived two years. You remember his siblings who were at the shop that day we adopted him. They had passed away within a month only. So we couldn't have done anything dear."

"Yeah. Let's talk about something else now... please." She said, still crying.

After some time, when all of them were a bit off the subject, she went to the other room and cried the hell out... Everything she hoped all these years, everything she prayed for was all shattered in no time. It was all based on a lie. Her whole world had turned upside down...everything she believed in, everthing she hoped for was based on nothing but a lie...

CHAPTER ELEVEN

KACY'S JOURNAL

10th March, 2020

Tuesday

Dear Diary,

Since 4 days, I've been having these dreams about Ronnie. I swear 4 days in a row. In some, he was talking to me somehow and in some of those, he was still a puppy. I don't know if it's a sign, or I'm just missing him a lot lately. And even if it's a sign, I don't know what it's for. I know I've told you a lot about him and it gets boring sometimes but I don't know how I'm supposed to just forget him. I've been thinking a lot about him lately and today I finally decided to search a bit about his disease. It turned out that the infection that he had is normal in Labradors breed dogs. And it's not deadly. What if Ronnie is cured and they didn't tell us about it? I miss him a lot. I know I was just 8-9 when I lost him and now I'm 13. And it's been 4-5 years since then. I don't know how I'm supposed to let him go. I still start crying when I get reminded of him too much. And because of that I have been trying not to think about him that much. I don't even know what happened to him. I just want him back in my life, I don't know how, I don't know when. I would give anything to just get one moment with him. I miss him a lot... It's almost like I'm stuck between this whole thing where I miss him more than anything and where I don't even know what happened to him. I know that everyone wonders why I miss him so much even though I was 8 when he left. I know that everyone thinks that I don't remember much of him but that is so not true. I rememer everything. I just don't know why I'm still traumatised by that. Maybe because it was the first time I lost someone in my life. Or maybe because I don't know what actually happened with him. Maybe I just feel guity for not beig able to spend more time with him. Then again, why do I feel guity? Its not like it was in my hands to control the infection. I think the situation would be the right thing to blame...

You know, I still have his chair with me on the terrace. It has this texture on its arms because Ronnie scratched most of it and whenever I touch it, it reminds me of him and makes me feel kida good because it was his. So whenever I'm stressed about something or need to take my my off things I go to the terrace and sit on it and enjoy the fresh air. It always brings the sweet old memories back...

20ᵗʰ March, 2020

Friday

Dear Diary,

Today was one of the most unexpected days of my life. I found out what really happened to Ronnie 4 years ago. I just can't believe how Mom and Dad kept this from me all these years.

We were all sitting in their room having breakfast together right after waking up. Then Peter and I started talking about how we are ready to get a new pet dog and that we'll take care of him. We were talking about dogs so I decided to tell mom and dad how that skin disease is normal in Labradors and that it can be cured. Then I said so much that they got mad at me. Then dad told me to never talk about it again. Then a few moments later, he started telling me. When they reached the hospital, the doctors immediately said that the disease that Ronnie has is at a very severe level and that it could not be cured. They told dad that it was good that they brought him to the hospital or he would have passed away in front of our eyes. He said that there's nothing they can do about it and that eventually Ronnie is going to pass away in a week or two. And that death will be really painful for him. And it'll be painful for us too, to watch him that way. The doctor even scolded dad saying that the infection could've spread in the kids (Peter and I). So he suggested giving him an injection which would send him into a forever sleep without any pain. So that he could die a peaceful death. The way dad described everything got me chills and I just couldn't stop crying. In fact I'm crying right now while writing this. He said that the doctor and the nurses had tied Ronnie's mouth and legs and placed him on the table. He was looking at dad as he was going to take him back home to us. To his family.when he said this I just froze in shock. I didn't know what to do. I didn't know what to say. Dad's words had so much pain in them. I'm literally shivering while writing this. My dad who is the strongest person I've ever seen in my life was crying. Mom and even Peter started crying. Grandma was in the other room so she didn't know.

Then mom told me that when Ronnie was a few months old and they went to Pet Spot to buy some stuff, the shop keeper told him that Ronnie's siblings had passed away within a month or two because of some genetic problem. But we were lucky that Ronnie even survived for 2 years. Or he would've gone way too early. Call it a miracle or whatever but we were definitely lucky. Then again, I can't say lucky because its not normal to lose your pet when he's just two years old. And I just realised that he was just two when I counted from 2013 to 2015. It honestly never felt like it. I really thought it was more than that. Poor baby was just 2 when such terrible thing happened to him.

And I am so that grateful that I got to spend those two years with him. And I'm grateful that Ronnie didn't get sick as a puppy. I can't believe how mom and dad kept this from us all these years. I had always thought that Ronnie was out there with a nice family or something. But he passed away on the exact day we sent him to hospital. The exact day we said goodbye to him. And all these yeass since the day we sent him, I've been praying to God to cure Ronnie or at least let me meet him sometime, it was all for nothing. It never mattered. It only made things worse as I kept om hoping for nothing. The chances for my hopes to come true ended before they even began.I even got mad a couple of times because all these days, I have prayed every single night and nothing seems to work. So all these years I thought that he was out there somewhere but he was already gone. This is a lot to take in. Mom and dad shouldn't have kept this from me for so long. I've gone through a lot of pain because of this confusion about what would've happened and this came out of nowhere. All those years of hoping and praying, it was all for nothing. All these years of my life were based on a lie. I think if they told me earlier, it would've been a bit easier to take in but now that 4-5 years have gone, I can't believe how hard it was for me. I have been hoping for something that was impossible to happen. I had come up with so many theories about what would have happened but none of them were even close to what actually happened. When they falsely told about that contract thing, I thought that okay, atleast he might have some new friends to keep him busy from remembering us...

Mom and dad said that they never told me about this because I got really sick just for leaving a house. How was I supposed to handle the lost of Ronnie? I can't even blame them.

They did what they thought was right for me. And they even asked me if I wanted to get a new one, but I always felt that it would mean that I'm replacing Ronnie or betraying him.

I just hope that wherever he is right now, in heaven, or the afterlife or even if he's in another life, I want him to know that I love him more than anything. And that I will never ever for get him. I hope his soul rested in peace. I hope he didn't feel betrayed. And I hope that the injection didn't hurt. I hope he didn't know what the doctors were doing to him and what was about to happen. I want him to know that his family has not forgotten him and will never forget about him. I want him to know that those 2 years were the best ones of my life and that we all love him more than anything and will love him forever...

13ᵗʰ September, 2020

Monday

Dear Diary,

Remember when I told you how I've started writing songs lately. Well the second one I wrote was probably in March or April. It was called "Wait for you" and I wrote it for some celebrity crush of mine. Who also happens to play Spider Man. I've probably written a lot about him and I'm not willing to talk about that today.That was the first song I wrote with chords. After that I've written several songs.

But today, I finished writing the first song I ever 'wrote'. By 'wrote' I mean I was aware that I was 'writing' a song. Because technically the first song I 'made' was the one I made for mom to convince her to let me wear my raincoat in the house. I was probably 4-5 back then and it was my new raincoat so I had a weird obsession with it but the buttons were really tight so I had to ask mom to open them for me. Anyways, so the song I finished today is called 'The Light of My Life'. I had written the chorus in the end of 2019 I guess so technically that was the first song I actually 'wrote'. And guess what, I wrote it for

Ronnie. It was just a chorus before and today I added 2 verses in it. Because today is his birthday maybe. I'm 70 percent sure that it's today but i don't know. Mom's not telling me.

Anyways, so here it is:

Verse: You know I've always loved you

Even though I couldn't prove it

'Cause I never thought I could lose you

And what we had was perfect

When I look back at those memories

Every moment is worth a tear

Wish I could get it all back

I still feel like you're here

Pre-chorus: Wish I could build a time-machine

And live back all of those memories

And even if I cannot do it

I just want you to know that

Chorus: I miss you

I need you

I want you

Back in my life

And I don't know

How i survived without you

'Cause just as the Moon need the Sun to shine

I'll always need you by my side

'Cause you were the Light of My Life...

Verse 2: Still remember my last day with you

You were right there in my arms

Didn't know I was losiing you

Thinking about it hurts so hard

(Repeat Pre-chorus)

(Repeat Chorus)

So this was it. It doesn't show the melody so you can consider it as a Poem/Song.

I know its not that good as its one of my firsts. But it has a special place in my heart than my other songs because it means a lot to me. I still haven't shown this to anyone else because I'm a bit consious about it because I don't want anyone to ruin it by judging or questioning why I write songs. Trust me, it has happened a lot of times and I didn't like. But I'll show them eventually...

CHAPTER TWELVE

New Car!?

It took a lot of time for Kacy to get used to the truth. After a lot of tears and a lot of overthinking, she felt a bit better. Better than those horrible four years. At least now she knew the truth. So she didn't have to keep on thinking and wondering about it all the time. And the fact that Ronnie went peacefully made her feel better. But the fact that he was gone traumatized her. But it was better than to live behind a rock of lies.

A few months later, the A.C of their car had started acting up. And every single time they sent it to the garage to get repaired, it worked correctly for a few days and started acting up again. After getting it fixed for almost 5-6 times they finally realised that instead of spending money on that car now and then, it was a better idea to just get a new one and sell the other one back.

Kacy was fourteen now and a freshman in high school. Peter was in 6th grade.

It was the 13th of November, 2020. The family was all hyped up to go to the showroom and finally get their new car. Mom, dad and grandma woke up at 6 AM. in the morning. Dad got ready first because he had to go to the bus station with Matt and Aunt Beth to get some delivery. He left at 7 AM after waking up the kids. They immediately got up and started getting ready because they were really really excited.

"Where did dad go?" Kacy asked.

"I don't know, Aunt Beth called, she said that Matt had ordered something. And they had to go and get it because the delivery was going to come at the bus station." Replied mom.

"Oh, okay."

When he got home, all of them except were on their way to the showroom. When they stopped at the traffic light, Kacy was looking out of her window and she saw a little pug with his owner. It was so adorable. And his legs were so little. And it melted Kacy's heart. She immediately spoke up, "Hey look that doggie is so cute! I can't believe I've never played with a pug before." Peter then tried to look at it but the green light had started and dad had started the car.

When they finally reached the showroom, the excitement just got more and more. When they entered, there were almost 30 new cars all lined up and of the same brand. One of them was of the Snows. It was really hard to figure out which one was theirs but it was no big deal because the paper work was still left. They went inside the and the manager came.

"Good morning Mr. Snow. Welcome. I see you're here with your family. Your car is all ready we can go see after I get some signatures for the paperwork."

"Okay let's go then."

"I'll get the papers." saying this, he went inside the office.

While they were waiting for the manager, they decided to click some photos in the showroom itself. And a few moments later, the manager came back.

It took almost 15 to 30 minutes to finish the paperwork. Then... it was time to finally get the new car. The manager took the family to where their car was. One of the workers was sticking a ribbon on the car and then it was finally ready. The shiny white colour. With wide space inside, wider than their old car. The grey leather seats and the smell of a brand new car. Their fourth one. It was amazing

Then the manager clicked some photos of the family with their new car. Then the manager and dad were having some discussion.

Then they left the shoowroom in their brand new car and went to the *temple* where they decided to do the *pooja* of their new car. They were waiting for the *pandit* to come when, Kacy's eyes fell on a little litter of newborn puppies under a bench. They were so small and adorable. Probably 10 days old. She showed them to Peter.

"Mom, look there's a litter of puppies. They are so adorable."

When mom saw those, her heart also melted. "Aww... they are so little."

"Can I please take one in my hands?"

"You need to ask your dad for that."

"Dad?"

"Yeah you can play with them after we're done with the *pooja*, okay?"

"Okay."

Then the *pandit* came and said that his shift in the other *temple* had already started and asked the Snows if they were okay if they did thwe *pooja* there. Mr. and Mrs. Snow said yes. So they went and did the *pooja* there.

Then they were on their way home. "Our new car is more spacious than the old one. And it's really comfortable too. I love it!" Kacy exclaimed. "I love it too!" Peter added.

"Well I didn't get to play with the puppies."

"Don't worry, there are a lot of puppies in the world, not just those. Who knows if there's a new litter in our neighborhood."

"No dad, there's not a single puppy in our neighborhood. If there was, I would've known."

"Well then just pray to God that you want to play with puppies. Maybe he'll listen today itself." said mom.

"Really mom?" Kacy said sarcastically.

"Yeah just do it."

"Fine." She herself didn't know why she said fine. Mom and dad were being really weird. Kacy didn't know why they were being so confident while saying that. She thought that how can a puppy miracally come in their neighborhood? They were acting really suspicious. But she ignored that.

When they finally reached home, dad parked the car right in front of their house to show it to Aunt Beth and Matt (who was 21 now) . While they were entering, dad shouted, "How is that Bean bag that Matt ordered? Where is it?" Kacy went inside with dad and Peter. When she entered the living room, she was looking for the Bean bag which dad was talking about. But instead of that, there was a little brown and white cushion kind of thing with little chew toys on it. She didn't know what was going on. Why were they dog toys on that bed? Why would Matt order this? She was still walking behind dad and Peter and then suddenly Matt opened the door of his room. She just froze while she was halfway there. In the middle of kitchen and Matt's room. She just stood still without saying a word. It was so little, so cute. There was a Labrador puppy walking and tumbling near the door of the room. As soon as Peter saw it, he just ran and and started playing with it while Kacy stood still with her hands on her mouth and in complete shock as if her heart started running as fast as it could go. It was like the whole moment just froze and she had no idea what was going on. It felt so surreal. Tears rolled out of her eyes and she didn't even know it. When she first saw it, she took a few steps back. Couldn't believe her eyes. Then dad turned to Kacy, looked at her with teary eyes and went straight into a hug. Both were crying. Kacy couldn't even breathe.The whole moment was so surreal. Then they stopped hugging and the little puppy came towards Kacy.

Still having tears roll down her cheeks, she took the puppy in her hands and came into the living room. She was shivering because she cried so much. The puppy fit right in her hands. It started licking the tears off Kacy's face. And that made her cry more. She loved the puppy smell. It reminds her a lot of Ronnie. Puppy smell is the best. This was the first time she saw a Labrador puppy in person after Ronnie. She whishpered in a low voice, "Ronnie." without even realising that wasn't him. Her desire of all these years had come true in the most unexpected way. All she wanted was to feel Ronnie once again. And she felt that with the puppy.

Then Aunt Beth came and asked "Why's she crying? Oh! Don't cry dear, your Ronnie is back." Kacy smiled and glanced at the puppy with her watery eyes. Then her eyes were laid on that cusion with dog toys. "Was this the parcel?" she asked in a shivering voice.

"Yeah" said Matt. "We ordered him from a YouTuber. He sent him from the northern side. The delivery guy came all the way from there in a bus with the puppy in a little basket."

"What are you going to name him?"

"Well like father, like daughter. Your father had the same reaction at the bus station when we went to get him. Instead of sitting at the driver's seat, he sat at the backseat and took the puppy in his hands and called him Ronnie instinctively. He was crying just like you. Yeah your dad's not as tough as he claims to be. Here, look at the video." Aunt Beth said while holding out her phone to Kacy.Then she gave out a giggle while watching dad's reaction. "What are we going to name him?" she asked.

"Ronnie!" said Matt. And everyone's face lit up with happiness. "Ronnie Jr." Kacy interupted. Then mom took him in her hands, she also looked extremely happy and emotional. She also had tears her eyes and felt like she was holding her Ronnie. All of the memories came back somehow. It felt like they went back in time. It was amazing.

In the evening, Aunt Rose, along with Molly and Kevin, came to meet the newest little member of their family. Ronnie Jr. was just month old. He almost slept the whole day as he was exhausted. And why wouldn't he be, he did travel miles and miles for days in nothing but a little basket. And in a bus. When he fell asleep for the first time, Matt lifted him up and kept him in his new bed. Yes the one that looked like a cushion. Then he immediately woke up and started crawling in the corners of that bed. And when he finally figured that out, he just climbed out of it and fell asleep on the floor. Matt tried putting him to bed several times but every single time, little Ronnie would just come out of it and sleep on the floor. After a few tries, he let it be like that.

While he was sleeping, Kacy took a pillow and placed him right beside him and laid there. Just like the time she did in 2013. When Ronnie was there. She didn't even realise that until she touched Ronnie Junior's fur and got a flashback of the good old days.

In the evening, when Ronnie finally woke up from his long sleep, Dad showed him a toy and everyone started calling him. And when he tried to walk towards them, his little legs just slipped in the four different directions. The tiles were too smooth for his soft paws that he couldn't even walk straight. Everytime someone took him in their hands, he would just start biting their fingers with his little pointy teeth. And when he finally got a chew toy in his mouth, he barked. For the first time in front of the family. It was so adorable.

And as Ronnie slept the whole day, he stayed awake all night till 2:30 AM. Peter and granma were asleep. So only Mom, Dad, Matt and Aunt Beth were awake with Ronnie. Peter sure was going to be mad if he found out that they got to play with Ronnie junior at night. Because he waited so much for him to wake up. But the real energy of Ronnie jr. was seen at night when he was all refereshed. Sometimes he would go to Matt, sometimes to Dad, then Mom and then Kacy. Sometimes still slipping with all his legs in all four directions. It was really funny. Aunt Beth was still keeping a bit distance but she'll get used to it within a few weeks.

After playing for almost an hour, Ronnie Jr. finally fell asleep. And Mom, Dad and Kacy were also ready to go to bed. This had been one of the best and the most unexpected and surreal days of Kacy's life. This happiness was a bit different than winning medals and trophies. It was so much more than that. She was now able to sleep peacefully. And now her whole life was back on track. Words cannot describe her feelings...

CHAPTER THIRTEEN

Deja Vu

13th December,
Sunday
Dear Diary,

It's been a month since Ronnie Jr. came in my life. He's two months old now. And has grown a bit since last month. I'm really happy that Matt adopted him. I'm really grateful of him for that. It has even brought us a bit closer than we were before. So yeah our bro-sis relationship is bonding. Its like a blessing to my whole family that Ronnie Jr. is there with us now. Because after our Ronnie passed, it was really hard for all of us to go through that loss. Each of us went though it differently. For some of us, it took just a few months but for some of us it took years. And some are still trying to deal with it. And by that I mean me. I mean its better than how it was before, before I was just a confused little girl who didn't know anything. But after I found out the truth, it gave me some kind of peace. At least now I don't have to keep wondering how Ronnie must've been. I didn't even know what euthanasia meant before dad told me about it. I didn't even know that the vets could do that to pets to give them a peaceful forever sleep. And you know it was that time when I realised that Ronnie was just 2 years old when he passed away. Till then I thought that I spent almost 5-6 years with him. It felt quite unbelievable at the moment but then I counted the years from 2013 to the year when I was in 4th grade which was 2015. Its funny how to get attached to something in just 2 years and when they're gone, it kills you from the inside.

Speaking of 2013, I just figured out that 13 is a lucky number for my whole family. For starters, my first house was C - 13. So was Peter's. Ronnie was born on 13th September, 2013. See again with the thirteens. And our new car and Ronnie Jr. came on 13th of November. Which was also Friday the thirteenth, I just realized that, whatever. All the digits in our car's number adds up to 13. I wrote my first song when I was 13. It's insane. Now I know what to say if someone asks me my favourite number. I'm still not sure about my favourite colour though. I guess it depends on my mood.

Alright, so... as I was saying, Ronnie Jr. is really adorable. Really naughty. And you know, he has a tendency to chew every single thing that fits in his mouth. Whenever I take him in my hands, he starts biting my fingers. At the beginning it seemed cute and was a little ticklish but now that his teeth are growing, it hurts. So it's better to keep a chew toy with me. But I don't what obsession he has with fingers, even if I show him his favourite toy, he'll first go for my fingers. Hahah... And no matter how many toys we buy him, he finds the houshold stuff more interesting than them. One day we brought him a rubber toy which made sounds if moved. There was some stuff inside it. He sniffed it a little bit and then started playing with the box in which we put our chess pieces. And the excitement he has while playing with it is insane. Because it's a cylindrical shaped box with blue lid and transparent body. So it keeps on rolling. And it's too big to fit in his mouth so everytime he tries to bite it, it keeps on rolling. Sometimes he even gets furious at it. But it never seems to bore him. He is so little and whenever he gets angry at the box it's really adorable to watch.

He also has an obsession with dads keys. Whenever he sees it, he gets so excited. Well, whenever he sees dad, he gets excited. Dad puts his keys in his pocket and Ronnie has somehow noticed that. So whenever dad's playing with him, he first goes near his pocket and fits his face inside it. It is so adorable. And it happens every single time. Dad has also taught him to jump. He just shows him the keys and then holds it on top of him. Then he jumps. It's always so fun to watch him.

Apart from his naughtiness, sometimes he does things that just melt my heart. Whenever my younger cousins and Peter are playing with him and I'm waiting for my turn while sitting on a chair or the couch, he would just come near my legs and sleep whenever he's tired. Mom and Dad say that he feels safe like that. Aww... I don't think anyone has ever felt safe with me before. He would just keep his head on my feet or just take support beside it. His fur is so soft. I love him. And if I'm not sitting on a chair or a couch, and just sitting on the floor with my legs folded, he would just come and sleep on my lap. It feels so good. It warms my heart. Ronnie Jr. is really adorable.

One day when Ronnie fell asleep after playing, Peter and I decided to play chess till he woke up. We had just started playing. It was Peter's turn and he was taking a lot of time so I decided to check up on Ronnie Jr. Because I remember in 2013,the last time I took my eyes off Ronnie, he had gone near the bathroom and was sniffing everything. So when I looked back at Ronnie Jr. a few days ago. He had woken up and was sitting still, looking right at me as if he was thinking, "Why is Kacy not playing with me?" Then Peter an I immediately stopped playing chess and went to Ronnie.

You know, Peter doesn't remember much about our Ronnie. Because he was really little when we had him. Well he does remember that day when we were playing at the quarters while dad was walking Ronnie. He had tripped and the Ronnie immediately ran under him so that he does not fall. I know it sounds a bit unbelievable but it was real. I remember it all too well. He also remembers the day we went to Pet Spot.

Just because now we have Ronnie Jr., it doesn't mean that I've forgotten my Ronnie. I still miss him terribly. Ronnie Jr. is nice but there was something different with my relationship with Ronnie. Maybe because Matt has adopted him or I don't know. It doesn't make any sense. I have probably spent more time with Ronnie Jr. than Matt himself has this whole month. Ronnie has left an empty space in my heart that cannot be filled by anyone. Not even an identical looking puppy who's name is also the same. I love Ronnie Jr. more than you can imagine but Ronnie meant something more,something different. He is and will always be a part of me.

And if you're out there somewhere, maybe in afterlife, maybe in heaven or even if you're reborn. I hope you're happier than ever. I hope you're around people who are better than us. And I'm really sorry if we couldn't take care you correctly. I just want you to know that we haven't replaced you, Ronnie. And we would never ever replace you. Even an identical looking puupy with the same name cannot replace you. And I promise you I will take care of him.You'll always be a part of us. I love you more than anything I've ever loved. You were a gift to me and our family. And no one in this world can ever take your place and don't you ever forget that. You were a blessing to us and thank you so much for being so good and so loving. You're my life. You're the reason for me to keep going. You are the reason why I have achieved so much in my life. You are everything I've ever wanted and I'm grateful of you to be in my life even though it was just for two years. I just wish you stayed for some more time to see how our practice made me win my first medal. And several more after that. I can also call them our medals and our trophies. And how I wrote my first song for you. My first poem. It was all for you Ronnie. You are the best thing that has ever happened to me and don't you ever forget that. You are and will always be the Light of my Life. I love you. And I will love you Always and Forever. And I'll never forget you...

From The Author

To my fellow readers... I'm Sneha Chaudhary. You might have figured that out by the cover of this book. I'm a fourteen year old from the westernmost part of India. I was born on 1st November 2006. By the time you read this, depends on the year, I may be 15 or 18 or even older. I don't know how many people are going to read this book after knowing that it's been written by a fourteen year old.

This is the first novel I've ever written. And it's basically a non-fiction one because I've written it based on my life experience. Everything you read in this book has happened in reality to my family and me. Except for the names. But Ronnie and Ronnie Junior's names were real. So basically Kacy is me, Peter is my brother and so on...

I've written it from a third person's perspective. The only thing that you'll read from my perspective, in this book, is the Journal chapter, the last chapter and this 'From the Author' column. Everything that included "Dear Diary... and so on..." was from some of my old journals. Ronnie Jr. is here with me and my family. He has grown a lot since then. And yeah, not all of my family members are mentioned here just because I didn't want to confuse the readers.

This novel was originaly published on 17th October, 2021 but the publisher to whom I sent the manuscript to didn't deliver the books to India so I had to find some other publishing company to finally get the paperback version of my book. So I decided to write a little bit more in this part of the book and fill you in with some thing that happened after 17th October, 2021.

On 26th December, 2021, we brought home the newest member of my family. His name is Jackie and he's an adorable little German Shepherd. He was 35 days old when we brought him home. And unlike Ronnie Jr., this little one lives with us. And... to be honest, I felt the déjà vu thing more with Jackie than with Ronnie Jr. because he lives with us and I spend every single day with him. We even made him sleep in that blue basket bed that belonged to Ronnie.We used it the same way we did with Ronnie, we also used it to block the way between the kitchen and the living room so that he doesn't go wanderig to the places like the bathroom and all. If you've read the whole book, you might be knowing about it. Its been 5 months with Jackie and it has been amazing. He's really a precious little being and also a blessing to me and my family and we love him more than anything. When we introduced him to Ronnie Jr. for the first time, the funniest thing happened. Little Jackie started running after him and he got scared and started running away from him. Now, 5 months have passed and still it's the same thing but instead to running, Jackie has started jumping around him and trying to get him to play but Ronnie Jr. barely likes to go for his walks so he ends up being annoyed. So poor Jackie is never able to convince him to finally play. But both of them get really jealous whenever the other one gets more attention from dad. So its always a challenge for him to be with either one of them whenever they are in the same room. Jackie always gets anxious when anyone from mom, dad, my brother or me goes outside the house. He starts barking in an angry but also emotional sort of way. And whenever anyone of us is not at home and he misses them, he starts howling. Its just so sweet. Due to which, now we always try our best to take him wherever we go. This time the experience is a bit different than with labradors. He is way smarter than we are and always ends up tricking us, whenever my parents try to scold him, he simply goes over and sits on their lap to emotionally blackmail his way out, privacy is not an option,he follows us around everywhere, loves sitting on the couch with us, and a lot more...but no matter how energetic and playful he is, he always stays disciplined. There hasn't been a single time when he has ever bitten or scratched any of the furniture or any other household item, unlike labradors, hahah. But most importantly,he never fails to show that he loves us and it's the sweetest thing ever. There's something about him that has been able to fill the emptiness our heart had after Ronnie and we are really grateful for that. After all, a new dog never replaces an old dog, it merely expands the heart in the most beautiful way...

When I first found out that Ronnie was euthanized, I didn't believe it that vets could do that. In fact, before I didn't even know that it was even a thing. So I started researching about it and learnt at almost 52.6% of pets get euthanized every year. And that really broke my heart knowing that so many pet owners have to go through that. The hardest part, for pet owners is not the playfulness or barking or cleaning up after them, the hardest part is the goodbye. It kills you from the inside. A part of you gets lost leaving emptiness in your heart. And their absence doesn't feel real. It's like your whole world has tuned upsidedown. And to anyone who has ever lost a pet in any sort of way, I wish you strength and I hope you remember the best memories you had with them instead of sorrowing over the terrible truth. Your pet is always looking down at you from heaven and loves seeing you happy. They are always going to be there with us no matter where they are...

The only reason I wrote this novel is because I wanted to remember every single memory I had of Ronnie. First I thought of writing it in a journal just so that I could look back at it after I grow up. Then I thought, "I could always make it as a novel! That would be cool. It'll be like a memoir for Ronnie. Plus I would get to share it with others."

So here it is. And I'm really grateful. Thank you so much for reading my debut novel and for letting me share my experience with you. It really means a lot...